Stories of Halabja Chemical attack in March 1988 and the Anfal Genocide Campaign

When 182000 civilians Kurds were shot or buried alive in various parts of South Iraq

Preface

I was in London when Halabja chemical attack happened on 16th March 1988 the day after as I was going to work, I saw on the London newspapers pictures of my town, my uncles house, where many were suffocated to death with nerve gas, Cyanide, Sarin, amongst thousands killed were two families of my cousins all murdered, with many friends, and neighbours. They were all civilians, had no part in politics of war and revolution.   This was the crime of Genocide, ethnic cleansing, mass slaughter in late 20s century, it was Pan Arab Nationalism's final solution.

Introduction

Halabja is a medium-sized town in South Kurdistan, north-eastern Iraq with a population of about 110,000 people, set on high ground at the eastern end of the Sharzour plain, near to the Iranian border. It is approximately 75 km from the Kurdish regional city of Slemani. It has an altitude of about 726 metres and average rainfall is 750 mm per year. It is surrounded by three chains of mountains: Shnerwie at 2110 metres high, northeast of Halabja; Balanbow, southwest of the town at about 1560 metres high; and the Hawraman range, from the north to the southeast periphery of Halabja, at 2160 metres high.

At the southern end of Hawraman is the 2548-metre high Surein mountain. The Sirwan river streams down before the Balanbow, deep at the foot of the mountain and runs towards the Derbandikhan water dam and through the plain of Jalawla to join the Tigris river near Baghdad. Halabja is situated on a sloping, fertile arable plain; from all sides wheat and barley has been grown for about a mile, and from the southwest the land descends to the fertile Sharzor plain.

 Kur in Sumerian times meant 'mountain', and kurti meant 'mountain people' or 'tribe'. Gondwana meant the language of Kurds (in the Kurdish language, Gond means village). During the Assyrian period, South Kurdistan was a part of Mesopotamia called Zamwa, covering Sharzour up to the Zagros/Hawaraman Mountains and included Halabja, where the ancient remains of Assyrian barricades still exist, indicating where the Assyrians gathered their forces in their frequent military campaigns in the region.

The Medes, who were ancestors of the ancient Kurds, defeated the Assyrians in their capital of Nineveh in 612 BC and they established an empire that stretched the length and breadth of the Middle East for many years. The Persians intertwined with the Medes through intermarriage and then they defeated Asteyages, the last king of the Medes, in battle. This led to the establishment of the Persian Empire.

The Medes Empire came about because the Assyrians kept coming to demand levies and taxes from the Kurds, which they always refused. The Assyrians came every two or three years with big armies to plunder, kill and burn Kurdish villages and towns. They often crossed the high, ragged mountains, going as far as Lake Urmyia on the other side of the Zagros Mountains in East Kurdistan (Iranian Kurdistan today).

This repression, plunder, looting and mass murder brought the Medes, or Kurds, together to form the biggest force in their history and destroy the Assyrian forces forever, with the destruction of their capital Nineveh (Mosul) in 612 BC.

After the Persian king, Koresh, defeated the last Median king, Astyages, the Persians went on to conquer most of the Middle East, going as far as India and Egypt, until the Sassanid Persian dynasty was itself overthrown through Arab conquest, leading to the conversion of the peoples to Islam during the 7th century AD.

In the 12th century AD, the historic Kurdish and Muslim leader Saladin Ayubi founded the Ayubid Empire in Egypt, embracing Syria, Lebanon, Palestine and Mesopotamia, and stretching to North Africa and the Arabian Peninsula up to Yemen.

Saladin united several nations and regions to join his campaign to repulse the European Crusaders who sought to occupy and plunder the Middle East in the name of their Christian religion. The Ayubid dynasty lasted for about 90 years until Bauber, a Turkish warlord, came with an army to defeat Salih, the last Ayubid king, and occupy Egypt. This paved the way for the establishment of the Ottoman Empire which endured until the end of the First World War in 1918.

When Britain and France, as the First World War victors, carved up the region, South Kurdistan was added to the newly established Iraq, with the condition that all cultural, civil, legal and human rights of the Kurds should be recognised and provided for in the Iraqi constitution. However, the Kurds were unhappy to be ruled by tribal Arabs and, when they revolted, the British Royal Air Force (RAF) bombed the city of Slemani with phosphorous bombs (weapons of mass destruction), killing many. The RAF was also deployed against the forces of Sheikh Mahmoud Barzenji and Mahmoud Khani Dizli, whose fighters managed to shoot down five British planes.

A League of Nations decision taken in Geneva on 6 January 1925 was sent to British officials in Iraq, stating: 'The League of Nations put forward a request, to The British Empire in Iraq to undertake responsibility for the security and observance of Law and Order in South Kurdistan'. It was intended for the League to monitor the legal and civil rights of the Kurds in the area under the 'protection' of the British Empire.

The people of Halabja and Slemani, especially the intellectuals, were jubilant at the League of Nation's decision. There were meetings, discussions and celebrations, as they thought that this decision was final.

One of these people was the governor of Halabja, a well-known poet called Ahmad Mukhtar Jaff from the tribe of Jaff in the Sharazour and Halabja area, who was on good terms with the British in Kurdistan. All like-minded people were happy and optimistic that the British would keep their promises and would not let them down, having rid the area of the repressive and backward Ottoman authority.

The news was followed by articles in local papers such as the 'Zyian' ('Life'), a local Kurdish newspaper, expressing the people's delight. There were also meetings, cultural activities and poetry evenings. Poems were written about the news, which seemed as if self-determination had been announced.

This encouraged cultural activities, including the use of the Kurdish language in schools and publications and the foundation of the Association of Kurdish Scientists and Intellectuals in 1926.

Many learned and well-known writers and teachers wanted to get involved and there followed a meeting of about 300 of the Kurdish intelligentsia in the main Sharawani, where the council met, in the regional city of Slemani. Money was collected and plans drawn up for future cultural activities. In Halabja, there were more meetings, fundraising for cultural activities and plans made to develop education and open schools and evening classes to eliminate illiteracy.

However, things did not turn out as promised by the League of Nations. In 1932, the Iraqi government was accepted as a member of the League and the British no longer had direct power over it. Laws were watered down or not implemented, and only a minority of the local ministers and government officials were Kurds.

Despite the attempts by Kurdish intellectuals and some prominent tribal leaders to lobby the Iraqi government and the League of Nations, they all turned a blind eye to the Kurds' demands. Despite many demonstrations and protests, no one from the regime would listen when the Kurds demanded their rights.

This situation continued until 1945 when the historic Kurdish Mahabad Republic was proclaimed in East Kurdistan (Iran), with the temporary backing of Joseph Stalin in the Soviet Union. Stalin's real motive was to pressure the Persian government into giving him a share of Iranian oil. When the Iranians agreed to this, Stalin withdrew his support from the Republic and left it isolated. The West supported the

Shah of Iran, who sent an army with tanks to destroy the Republic, which had lasted for less than a year, and execute its leader, Qazi Muhamad, and other members of its governing committee.

Kurdish leader, Mulla Mustafa Barzani, had come from Iraq to support the Mahabad Republic. After its defeat he managed to flee to Russia with 500 men, mainly members of his Barzani tribe. They were pursued by Iraqi, Iranian and Turkish forces but still managed to reach Russia and seek asylum. During this tumultuous period, the Kurdistan Democratic Party (KDP) of South Kurdistan was founded.

The KDP became very active in Halabja. The concept of political activity for the liberation of Kurdistan spread to schools, youth associations, trade unions, student unions and farmers' associations. There were frequent meetings, discussions and educational activities using Kurdish books, magazines, patriotic lyrics, songs and poems.

In 1954, the first Nawroz festival was allowed in the Kanyiaqulka district in Halabja. The festival was attended by many people, and watched by many police because of the state's fears of an uprising. In 1955, the Nawroz festival was held at the National Park of Halabja. However, it was never officially recognised by the regime as the Nawroz Kurdish national festival; instead they called it the 'Festival of Trees and Woods'.

On 3 March 1958, there was a mass march in Halabja, ordered by the KDP and calling for the election of Halabja's representatives. The organisers prepared a document formulating the demands of the people which were presented to King Faisal of Iraq, the parliament, the House of Elders, and the prime minister. Copies were also distributed to Baghdad's main radio station, newspapers and magazines to be published in Kurdish and Arabic.

This document stated:

We, the Kurdish Nation in Iraqi Kurdistan request all our civil and legal rights be recognised and respected by the Iraqi government: these rights which were approved by the League of Nations in January 1925 in Geneva; the declaration of Human Rights that was signed and accepted by the Iraqi government in 1932 when Iraq was accepted and recognised as a sovereign nation. We demand those rights to be included and observed in the new Iraqi constitution, for the Kurdish Nation to protect our national, civil and legal rights and to be concise and clear with its implementation.

But the Kurds' demands were refused. In July that year, the monarchy was overthrown by the Free

Army Officers movement and this paved the way for the Kurdish Aylul (September) revolution in 1961. Halabja was one of the centres where that revolution began.

1. 'Halabja in the Arms of History 'written in Kurdish language' by Mr Hakim Mala Salih, Shehap press, Halabja 2004   .13, 15, 19, 20

2. 'Saladin in his Time', P.H Newby, Phoenix press, Jan, 1983, 17, 19, 23

1. The Aylul / September Revolution

Article Two of the Iraqi constitution, adopted after the overthrow of the monarchy in 1958, states: 'Kurds and Arabs are partners in the Soil of Iraq, both with equal rights.' This article became like a strong pillar for the unity of Iraq. For the peace and stability of Iraq, it was vital that the Kurds had equal human rights with Arabs, along with political and cultural rights and that South Kurdistan be granted autonomy within Iraq. However, the influential Communist Party of Iraq considered such demands as an attempt at separation by the Kurds, and argued that a nationalist Kurdish political party would lead to the break-up of Iraq.

It was so strange for the communists not to accept the human right of Kurdish children to study in their mother tongue. They did not even want Kurdish men and women to have their own political parties or students' and farmers' associations, saying that such organisations were not needed since we were all citizens of Iraq.

It was to no one's surprise that the Soviet Union was using the Iraqi Communist Party as their puppet to meddle in Iraqi affairs for the purpose of promoting arms sales. In the years following the 1958 coup, the Soviets armed various Iraqi regimes to the teeth. The political stance of the Iraqi Communist Party led many young Kurdish men to abandon the communists and join the Kurdistan Democratic Party.5

In 1960, under pressure from Arab nationalists, Abdul Karim Qasim began to renege on Article Two and a policy of openness and democracy that included the concept of shared nationhood. He banned the publication of Kurdish newspapers and magazines, disbanded the administration of Kurdish education and rounded up many Kurds suspected of belonging to the KDP, the Kurdistan Democratic Party.

The government banned the recruitment of Kurds into the police and army colleges and academies; those Kurds already employed in these institutions were deported to the Arab areas of southern Iraq. The regime raised taxes on agricultural production in Kurdistan to twice the levels of the rest of Iraq. Although the Kurdish leadership tried to negotiate and resolve their disagreements with the government, it was to no avail and the prospect of war loomed.

It was ironic that the Arab nationalists, and especially the communists, who were often known to demand freedom and democracy for oppressed nations, were opposed to Kurds getting their basic human rights.

Abdul Karim Qasim's government started to use a policy of divide and rule. To encourage tribal conflict in Kurdistan, he financed and armed a few tribal property owners to fight against the KDP leadership. On 31 July 1961, the KDP leadership presented a written dossier to the Iraqi Government and tried to discuss the situation in order to avoid armed struggle and war. The regime's reply was to deploy the Iraqi Air Force on 9 November 1961 when it bombed the Barzan region and a few other parts of Kurdistan and he followed this with a military incursion into Kurdistan.

The regime used 120 aeroplanes to bomb many Kurdish villages throughout Kurdistan. It hoped this would ward off any armed rebellion. This terror was accompanied by the regime's media propaganda campaign against Kurds.*

*This was seen in 'Ahd Al Jadid', The New Era newspaper no. 478 on 20 July 1962, and again the same newspaper no. 600, and in Al-Ayiam. The Daily News newspaper, no. 59, on 22 June 1962, started their campaign against the demands of Kurds to respect their basic human rights within the Iraqi state.

But for the Kurds there was no way forward apart from the armed struggle, although this caused disaster, and not only for Kurdistan since the conflict also spread to neighbouring countries. There followed many years of revolution and two big wars involving the international community, causing millions of deaths, billions worth of damage, and untold misery and grief.6.

In 1961, the Aylul Revolution began. The town of Halabja was one of the main centres of the uprising. Early one morning, Sajid, as a seven-year-old boy, saw that the town's streets and the local market were crowded with gunmen of all ages wearing strips of golden bullets that zig-zagged their chests like grinning golden teeth. The younger men showed off their weapons with a swagger that said they were ready for the revolution. They were known as the peshmargas: the ones who would face death. These freedom fighters were prepared to die before everyone else to rescue the country from occupation.

Everyone wanted to get hold of a gun or even a dagger. The insurgents had all kinds of guns: revolvers, old guns like the British MK1, some German guns, and some that were already popular with Kurdish tribes, like the 'Bernau'. There were even hunting guns. Many men loved to show off their guns with pride, and they wanted to exhibit their readiness to fight and to die to liberate Kurdistan. This was a common attitude, and the people's mind-set developed because of their long history of revolutions, with episodes of uprisings and periodic rebellions and confrontations in all parts of Kurdistan. The occupiers had never considered listening to the Kurds' demands. Instead, a policy of occupation, slavery and subjugation was pursued with the utmost cruelty by the Arabs, Turks and Persian regimes, and the victors in the First World War contributed to a continuance of this oppression after the demise of the Ottoman Empire in 1918.

Therefore, the Kurds were often forced to take the law into their own hands when any chance arose, with the backing of the mountains their only saviour, to seek human rights and their legitimate self-rule.

The school curriculum was all in Arabic; young children had to learn this even though their language and culture had nothing to do with the Arabic language. It was an alien language, and the language of occupation, which they were forced to learn, both at school and in the army. Every 18-year-old male had to do 18 months or two years compulsory army service. There was no way to avoid this. There was no chance of getting a job otherwise and many Kurds had to do it in the harsh Arab desert areas stretching from Baghdad to south of Basra, close to the Kuwaiti border.

The compulsory army service was meant to train young men to be ready for wars. It seemed that this was what the tribal leaders wanted in order to strengthen their own positions. They knew they were not the legitimate representatives of all Iraqis, as was proven in the following years, especially when power was monopolised by the minority Sunni Arabs.

The Kurds were demanding that their areas be governed and maintained by their own people to apply the principles of human rights as set out in the 1948 Geneva Convention.

The hands of outsiders were always ready to creep in, with the help of some local tribal cronies. The Communist Party was the first political party in Kurdistan that stood against the KDP. Instead of nationalism they espoused the Marxist-Leninist ideal of internationalism and, therefore, there was bound to be friction. The communists championed the interests of the Iraqi state and opposed the Kurds' national rights because this was in the strategic interests of the Soviet Union.

According to the communists' concept of internationalism, the important conflict is not between nations and races but between different classes since the upper-class rich have always exploited the working class, the poor and the disadvantaged. For the communists, liberating the poor was in theory more important than Kurdish independence or self-rule. In reality, however, the communists were used by the regime to create cracks of division among the Kurds. The communist party naively fell into the Iraqi regime's trap, but their attempt was not successful, and they had no significant impact on the Kurdish revolution.

When the first clash happened between the KDP and the communist party in Halabja, young Sajid and his friends saw that many people were all going someplace to fight, carrying logs of wood. It made him question, 'why are they fighting? Why do these people want to fight each other? Don't we all want our freedom and autonomy?' He thought that what he was seeing was incredible.

Sajid watched in silence. There was no immediate reply from anyone as to why there should be violently opposing factions within the community. He had to wait for years to reach an understanding of the politics of the situation.

In a patriarchal society, the young had no chance to pose these kinds of questions, which were left to the grown-ups to discuss. The local culture suppressed women and the young, and only the male elders, tribal leaders, well-known men and religious leaders could speak out.

Young people would sometimes talk among themselves about the republic, Kurdistan, revolution, guns, aeroplanes, the Arabs and schoolbooks. They knew about the Kurdish peshmargas in the town. There was no doubt the kids were all interested in guns, and in learning how to shoot, fight and be heroes in the revolution.

Those who had relations – fathers, uncles, brothers and others – actively involved in the revolution were more familiar with what was going on, and the rest would listen, watch and learn. Soon, young people were to learn about the names and types of guns and weapons and their capabilities. Many times they watched scenes of conflict in the town. In virtual silence they shared in the preoccupations and anxieties, happiness and celebrations of their families and neighbours. They were to grow up with a different way of life, the life of revolution, and they started making replica guns from pieces of cane or wood, which they often played with in the dusty alleyways, taking opposing sides. They stretched out their arms like the wings of aeroplanes and, for bombs, dropped paper bags filled with fine soil.

This situation had a profound effect on the young, who got used to the fighting, shooting, screaming and killing, and the coming and going of T-55 Russian tanks, which made the ground shake beneath their little feet. They grew familiar with the heavy Doshka sub-machine guns on the tanks, and the Russian MiG-17s and -18s and British- and French-made fighter jets. These were tools of killing and destruction. The young generation had to get used to the fact that, for years to come in Kurdistan, these would be the new norms of life.

They would get used to seeing rows of shops torched, houses burnt, and neighbours and relatives killed. They were to grow up with the mentality of war and revolution, to witness terrible scenes and then hear from adults that those who had been killed were going to heaven, as if this meant it did not matter. All this shaped the cultural psyche, and young people learned to face and accept the worst and try to get on with their lives.

Someone like Sajid would ask, 'Why does anyone who was killed go to heaven?'

'Because they were innocent, they were shaheed (martyr),' came the reply.

Of course, those on the government side thought the same about their 'martyrs'. If only one had dared to say, 'It all depends on which side you were on, to justify that belief'.

With the start of the revolution, the government began setting up special police units, with plain-clothed agents, to watch people. They hired people, especially Kurds, to observe and report on what was going on. This was considered a disgraceful job from a Kurdish patriotic point of view.

An atmosphere of suspicion and division was fostered, undermining the harmonious social relations of local people. Within a few years, one had to be careful and watchful, and look twice before mentioning any topics forbidden by the laws of the occupation. Many people resented this new atmosphere.

People's attitudes were changing. Years before, when someone was murdered, for whatever reason, everyone who heard the news was upset and angry and they grieved for the victim. When the revolution started, attitudes gradually changed because there was so much killing, torture and capital punishment.

1.   A Modern History of Kurds, by David McDowal, 1998

2.   A.V Williams, Zoroastrian the ancient philosopher, New York 1954

Mary Boyce, Zoroustra, London 1979

3.   Dum Dum Castle published by Amolibros, April 2013 as eBook on amazon.co.uk

4.   Halabja in the Arms of History by Hakim Mala Salih, published in Halabja 2004 93–104

5. Kashkoli Basarhatm by Sheikh Ali pp. 20–25 published by Kamal publishing

Slemani, KRG 2013

6. The Genocide of Barzini people 1975–1980 pp. 236–238, Barzanyian in 20th Century by Rebuar Ramazan

Abdulla, first edition, KRG 2011

7. Jaffar 1974, 153; Libaridian 1987, pp. 203–204, Phillipson et al. 1994, 7 Uppsala University universitat 1999, 34–35

8. Kristiina Koivunen, The Invisible War in North Kurdistan, 25, 26 KRG publications 2012

Ethnic Revival:

Ethnic revival is one of the legitimate rights of any group of human beings who share the same gene pool and who share a history of experience, and have shared likes or dislikes, happiness and suffering formulated through living together and intermarriage. Their security is a matter for every individual to work for, and struggle to protect their own existence, when they are ready to cooperate to protect their survival or even to die for it, if needs be.

In the Aylul Revolution, it was shown that the Kurds were ready to die to protect their homeland. It was obvious that giving in to the occupiers' wishes and ambitions would end up with giving in to the despotic regimes' policy of subjugation and slavery. In addition, the regime's political intention ended up with the policy of ethnic cleansing, which was considered as a crime of genocide/race killing, like what happened to the Armenians in 1915 shortly before the Ottoman Empire collapsed and modern Turkey was established. That was the very first time in modern warfare that this policy was used on a massive scale to murder over a million Armenians while the world was watching silently.7

This was the same policy used in Nazi Germany to get rid of Jews and Gypsies, as the ruling elite considered them a threat to the state's unity and Adolf Hitler ordered the massacre of five million Jews in Germany and Eastern Europe.

According to Smith, cultural, social and political values play the most important role in the formation of ethnicity. In explaining ethnic revival, attention must be paid to the conjunction of culture and politics; economic development acts only as a catalyst in particular situations. Threats to linguistic and cultural identities can have a very strong potential to mobilise groups. Economic deprivation is only grist to the nationalist mill, but in itself, it does not generate ethnic sentiment or nationalist movement; deeper existential problems are involved. In most cases in the process of ethnic revival, culture manifestations were preceded by pre-existing cultural organisations or journals and newspapers.

The hatred that an ethnic group can develop against another group probably has less to do with competition per se and more with the risk of having to give up something of oneself, one's identity. It is a question of survival in a cultural more than a material sense. If members believe that the very existence of the ethnic collectivism is threatened, the salience of ethnicity comes to the fore.

(Alfredson 1996, 73; Kallen 1996, 116; Philipson et al 1994, 7 Skutnubb Kangas and Toukomaa 1976, 2; Smith A, 1981, 5, 13–14, 23, 44) 8.

A Life of Revolution in Halabja

The peshmargas were the freedom fighters, the ones who were ready to die before others for the freedom of Kurdistan. They often came to town to attack government forces and show that they were ready to fight. Sometimes, the fighting lasted all night and other times for a few hours before everywhere went quiet again, and Halabja returned to its usual peaceful midnight silence.

For the young, it was like a kind of entertainment, unless it got too dangerous and ugly. The combatants often threw grenades and small 'Hawan' bombs at each other and occasionally these strayed into the foreyards of houses to wound or kill unfortunate residents.

But people's religious beliefs would bring them some consolation. When they said, 'That is God's will', they meant, 'Without God's will, nothing would happen to anyone'. This idea helped them reassure themselves; it provided some comfort and kept them going.

In the early 1960s, when the government forces were not very strong in the town, the peshmarga gunmen would arrive in broad daylight, in the afternoon or early evening. As soon as they fired any gunshots, the shopkeepers all rushed to bring down the aluminium shutters on their shops. The collective grinding noise sounded like so many volleys of sub-machine gunfire.

The shopkeepers ran, desperate to get home, and there they kept listening and anxiously waiting in front their houses to see what would happen next.

The peshmargas sometimes stayed for a few days, and all the shops would remain shut because it was too dangerous for anyone to come to town from outside. This volatile situation damaged trade and affected the livelihood of Halabja and the surrounding villages. When a bigger government army came to Halabja, all the gunmen escaped and went into hiding in the mountains. The new force came with tanks, armoured vehicles and artillery. In addition, many Arab soldiers, police and Kurdish jash* (mercenary) troops accompanied them.

 * jash' is a reference to a donkey's infant, because in Eastern culture the donkey is considered as a stupid animal.

For the local people, this was another nightmare, because the new forces searched the town for any gunmen, for anyone left behind when the rest had escaped and gone to the mountains.

Government troops combed through the town. They picked on a few families suspected of being the relatives and collaborators with the gunmen and carried out arrests and beatings. This was an opportunity for the government's corrupt authority to plunder and rob ordinary people of their scarce savings, using the threat of arrest, torture and death.

It was even worse whenever the government forces had incurred a few casualties. Most of the time, the soldiers targeted places that the peshmargas might have used to shoot at government positions. These events took place in the early years of the revolution, in the early 1960s, when the government reaction was not as severe as it later became, and the revolutionaries were not causing many government casualties.

When groups of gunmen were around, especially at night, they were welcomed, offered warm food and given shelter. Sometimes, a few would stay in hiding for several days. Most stayed with their own families, friends or people they trusted, belonging to undercover revolutionary groups.

The general mind-set of the revolutionaries was that a gunman could stay wherever he wanted, because he had put himself on the front line to liberate Kurdistan. They thought no one should dare to deny them assistance, and any refusal was considered as treason towards their homeland.

They often collected money, clothes and food. They had undercover groups within the community who voluntarily worked for them, collecting information on government activities and on Kurds who collaborated with the state. Some people, whether they liked it or not, could not express their real opinions. Many became resigned to how life was, though they would have preferred a more ordinary existence, and they did not get involved in any political argument to avoid trouble.

Sajid was a young man, with his family of five all sleeping in one room in winter, because they could only afford to warm one room with wood coal. This room had a little window next to the door. Their home was made of mud brick and roofed with wood shafts and the ceiling shafts were blackened by years of smoke from the coal tray. There was a small kerosene lamp hanging on the wall. Electricity did not come to Halabja until the late 1950s and still only a few people could afford it in their homes.

In this room a few framed verses of the Koran called 'Ayet al Kurssi' (verses for protection) hung from the walls along with pictures of the shrine of the prophet and a photo of Byiara Naqshbandi Sheikh. Sajid's father was one of his followers.

In winter, they all huddled around the fire tray, waiting for father to tell one of his stories about his travels to Baghdad. It was exciting for the children to hear about train journeys from Mosul or Kirkuk to Baghdad, because they had never even seen a train. As the regime often explained, 'The area is mountainous and it is difficult to bring train lines to Kurdistan.'

Kids were used to learning the Quran by heart before going to school. Like most of them, Sajid understood hardly a word of it. On cool summer mornings he used to go to the Khanum mosque with other children for about 90 minutes. Sajid's father paid the lame Mullah Ahmed six dirham per month for his tuition.

For Sajid it provided a sort of entertainment to mix with the other kids reciting the Quran in a choir. It was fun, like singing with his friends in the orchards and valleys. They also became familiar with the alphabet and some developed rudimentary pre-school learning skills. In Islamic culture, learning by heart was the traditional way of learning. It didn't matter whether you understood it or not and there was no attempt to explain the Quran to the kids. 'It was like blind education and perhaps the mullah himself didn't understand it,' Sajid later mused.

Sajid and some of his friends became more sceptical as they grew older. They wondered, for example, why some religious people would often say, 'This life is a test and, whatever happens, people should not forget God, as God is the ultimate power behind anything that happens in the world.' They argued amongst themselves about this. 'If God was behind whatever happening; why all the killing, fighting and destruction?' They would question how the almighty God could have a hand in such evil.

Sometimes they had long discussions with no clear conclusion, as though the answers were waiting, suspended somewhere. They often felt puzzled, because nobody came up with an answer to satisfy everyone, and they were young, immature and not yet well educated. In later years, Sajid and others could search for answers through their studies. But when they were still very young, they could only draw on practical experience.

As this new generation grew up, some sensed a big gap between the realities of life and the idealism of religion. When people were poor they had to work hard to survive. They needed to feed their families and no one had ever seen God drop a single loaf of bread to anyone, even if they were starving to death.

 However, religion was often the only source of comfort for people who might otherwise go mad with anxiety. It gave people a sort of relief, whether they believed in it or not. The majority were true believers, accepting that nothing would happen without God's will. For them there were the religious texts to use as a kind of guidance. If they didn't have that sort of faith, they might have butchered each other and plundered each other's properties. Their belief system moderated the actions of the majority and brought them comfort. It brought people together to share their grief and the burdens of difficult lives during the revolution.

From the mid-1960s the young increasingly talked about the conflict. They lived it every day. Sometimes their schools came under fire and they were haunted by the threat of abuse, arrest, bombings, stray bullets and being murdered. This was not just a physical threat; it also caused people psychological damage.

So did the cruel system of education. When Sajid finished his sixth year of primary school and went into the first year of secondary school, the whole school curriculum changed from Kurdish to Arabic. That was another type of psychological assault. The kids knew nothing about the Arabic language and culture, but none of the adults seemed to care. No parent would dare to raise the issue. No religious leader ever mentioned this kind of unfairness in their Friday prayers, due either to their ignorance or to intimidation from the regime. This was a policy of linguicide within the state's campaign of genocide: an enforced campaign to kill the Kurdish language and culture.

For many of the new generation, this created a culture of fighting back and resistance. They encountered a few opposing groups, like the communists and families of the landowners, who thought that the occupiers were their comrades and brothers. Often arguments started. 'Why should they run our country and force us to learn Arabic? We should teach them the Kurdish language if they are happy with our brotherhood?!' That was the view of many young men and women.

In one of the first clashes between the peshmargas and the state, Kurdish forces occupied the Derbandi Khan tunnel for a while and the Iraqi government used the air force for the first time. Russian MiG fighter planes attacked the area surrounding the tunnel and then they came to bomb Halabja. There were a few casualties on both sides but the peshamrgas' weaponry was too basic and they could not resist for long and had to withdraw.

Most of them later returned to the town and there were lively discussions about what to do next, how to reinforce their lines and resist the government forces. It was the first defeat the revolutionaries had experienced, and the young fighters were sad.

It did not take long for the peshmarga forces to grow stronger and start acquiring more up-to-date weapons such as the AK 47 'Kalashnikov', the Smirnov, and hand-held grenades called 'Rumana' in Arabic because they were the size of small pomegranates. They got hold of Bren sub-machine guns and Kalashnikovs from Kurdish soldiers deserting the Iraqi army and also from successful ambushes.1.

The Kalashnikov or AK47 gun was invented by a Russian army engineer, Michael Kalashnikov, in 1947. This was the first and most effective anti-personnel gun invented in the 20th century. It is estimated that more than half a million people have been killed by Kalashnikovs.

It did not take too long before they had set up a radio station to broadcast daily news of the struggle from somewhere in the mountains. As the revolution spread throughout South Kurdistan, this station gave updates on their daily operations. They also used wireless communication equipment seized from the Iraqi army. The revolution's leadership command centre was based in the faraway mountains and it organised a network of political and military groups, including secret cells operating among the civilian population.

The radio station became the mouthpiece of revolutionary propaganda. It was illegal to listen to it and if anyone was caught tuned in, they would be punished.

Every day, news of the revolution was discussed in the schools, tea shops and mosques. There were government secret agents operating in the community but still people talked openly to those they trusted. Of course, the government agents were hated and excluded from social gatherings and discussions if they became known. In the early years of the revolution, the regime used Arabs who could not speak and understand the Kurdish language. Gradually it managed to recruit some Kurdish spies, and it exploited tribal and local disputes to recruit jash mercenary fighters.

Secret cells of the revolutionaries were spied upon. If anyone was caught with documents proving their affiliation to the revolution they would be arrested, and they might be tortured to death or sentenced to capital punishment.

As the revolution continued there seemed to be no hope of negotiations. There were frequent clashes, including ambushes of army personnel on the roads and in the mountains. The army often incurred casualties and, when the troops came back to town, they unleashed their rage on ordinary people with beatings and shootings. They often tried to find the relatives of the peshmargas.

One time, when revolutionaries were staying in the town, the fighting went on for several days. The regime forces had posts in some taller buildings in town, including in a two-storey building near the centre, manned by several jash (Kurdish mercenaries). The peshmargas made a sustained attack and eventually overwhelmed this post. When they kicked the door open, they found several corpses on the upper and ground floors. They also found a few surviving jash who were trying to hide in the toilets. One tried to escape in women's clothes, but he was captured in the street. The revolutionaries were about to shoot him when a woman came out from a nearby house, shouting and holding a copy of the Quran. She pleaded with the revolutionaries to spare his life, because she feared government forces would come later to punish everyone living in the neighbourhood. As a rule, the revolutionaries did not kill any member of the army or jash who surrendered, on condition that they did not try to resist or escape.

Eighteen jash had been killed and local people were fearful that government forces would unleash their rage on civilians after the revolutionaries had left town.

Following the battle, Sajid watched as a group of women carrying guns came, shouting and screaming, to the town centre. They sprayed the shop fronts with a blue flammable liquid and fired on the shutters to set them alight. Sajid watched as so many shops were consumed by the flames. Columns of smoke turned the glaring sunshine into a gloomy dark spectacle.

These women had lost jash relatives in the previous days' shoot outs. They carried guns and were very angry, and no one dared to try and stop them. Many shops were burnt down, although the shopkeepers had nothing to do with the politics of the revolution.

As a young boy, Sajid watched the spectacle. He was no threat to either side. He watched the long rows of shops burning, their iron pillars and shutters crunching, twisting and melting in the intense heat. He saw how human grief and rage had culminated in this destruction, 'It is like Hell!' he suddenly thought, recalling his religious teaching. 'One couldn't for a moment resist the intense heat of hellfire.'

Sajid saw the father of one of his friends. This man was a victim whose shop had been turned into ashes. When he saw that the shop's structure was destroyed and all its contents turned to soot, he took out his handkerchief and started crying. But there was nobody to show any sympathy, share his despair or comfort him.

His shop was his livelihood, the product of many years of toil to feed his family of six. But there was no insurance and no one he could complain to or seek compensation from.

'How can God be so merciless and cruel?' thought Sajid. He knew that many people would tell the ruined shopkeeper, 'Don't worry, God will reward you in heaven after you die.' For the ordinary people, this was a new phase of the revolution, in which Kurds sometimes killed each other in horrific ways.

People who trusted each other might say, in a sad whisper, that this was against the spirit of the revolution. They could not freely express their views, because any expression of criticism or complaint about corrupt revolutionaries was considered as siding with the occupiers. The new atmosphere of doubt and uncertainty created an additional psychic pressure on the population. Many people would unconsciously make many changes, to fit in to the new community of revolution. The natural human instinct and compulsive desire for survival would drive people to make previously unimaginable decisions to manage their own security, to get power and to survive.

In any revolution or war, there will always be winners and losers. It would turn into a kind of business as, from both sides, there were people seeking to exploit the situation. The temptations of power and wealth could be overwhelming. Gaining power meant authority and having henchmen who were ready to commit any crime for the sake of money. Power meant overpowering others around you who had power or used to have power; power meant 'honour', sexual exploitation, greed and brutality.

The Iraqi government stepped up its attacks, once more sending Soviet-made MiG fighters to attack the Kurds, especially when the gunmen stayed in town for a few days, and Halabja was one of their very first targets.

The Soviet Union helped arm the Iraqi regime with the latest weaponry, including the MiG fighter jets, artillery pieces, armoured vehicles and T-55 tanks. The local communists still argued that the Iraqi regime was progressive and some even displayed glossy posters about the Soviet weaponry on their walls, arguing it was making Iraq strong against Western imperialism.

However, the Soviet Union's tools of destruction were used to kill the very same people who its leaders pretended to support and want to liberate from the claws of capitalism and imperialism. If one were to look at the Soviet Union's historical development, one would discover that, despite all the pretensions of emancipating the poor toiling peasants and workers, the true doctrine of Marxism was never implemented. It is an historical fact that, in Tsarist times, the landowners exploited Russian peasants like slaves. They thought they could use the peasants like commercial commodities, to buy and sell, and even rape and beat to death, punishing them and treating them like cattle herds. However, the principles of human equality, fairness and equal rights were never applied by the New Soviet Empire, which occupied and enslaved half of Europe for several decades.

The Bolshevik Revolution of 1917 was encouraged by Arthur Zimmerman of the Kaiser's Germany. Zimmerman sent Vladimir Ilyich Lenin in a sealed train via Sweden to lead a revolution and to make Russia pull out of the war in order to weaken the allied forces confronting Germany. He hoped this would help Germany win the war, but that part of his plan failed.2.

Halabja under Attack

In 1961, Russian MiG fighter planes of the Iraqi Air Force made their first appearance in the skies above Halabja. They came to attack the revolutionaries and threaten the population. They dropped bombs and fired on people using heavy Shastir ('60 arrows') sub-machine guns. Everyone, especially the children, were horrified by the scenes of explosions and collapsing buildings. As soon as the planes came, Sajid screamed and ran into the dark backroom of the house.

To Sajid, the aeroplanes were like dragons discharging colourful fire from their cockpits, with a crackling thunder. They were flying faster than the speed of sound, unloading heavy bombs and spraying sub-machine gun fire. It felt as though all the stars in the sky were clattering down on Halabja like heavy rocks. Sajid felt so scared and helpless that he ran indoors to hide, without waiting for the others, and after a while he fell asleep in the darkness of the backroom.

Eventually he awoke in the silent darkness, and suddenly remembered what had happened. He leapt to his feet and anxiously ran outside, pausing to check that his family were okay. They were fine. He looked up at the clear, blue sky. The sparrows were chirping noisily as usual. The birds on the big mulberry bush in the yard seemed unmoved by what had happened. For them life carried on without a hitch. 'How come they are not scared?' Sajid thought.

He kept thinking about what had happened, and those frightening and panicky moments. Many people became so scared during these attacks that afterwards there were queues in front of the shared toilets. Sajid learned that, at a time of intense fear, everyone worried about their own safety and that was why he ran in without looking to see what the others were doing.

People were advised not to stay indoors during the air raids in case their houses were bombed and fell on them. Everyone started to stay in their foreyards, huddled in tiny shelters built onto the fences, fearful of being torn apart by a bomb or by one of the plane's sub-machine gun bullets which were the length of an outstretched adult hand and more than an inch thick.

Sometimes the MiGs flew high above Halabja and released huge booms of noise. This was meant to frighten people because the government was waging a psychological battle against Kurdish civilians, many of whom had nothing to do with the revolution.

Whenever people went to work and the bazaar, or when children went to school, if there were any loud bangs they were ready to run for their lives. The easy atmosphere of the bazaar and the tea rooms, and of everyday social chitchat, changed as a constant sense of danger haunted the town.

Peshmarga gunmen often came to town, and people got used to this. Many shopkeepers then closed their shops earlier than usual, and the market centre and high streets became deserted from early afternoon. Many went home to be with their families or to the local mosque to wait and listen for news. There is a Kurdish proverb that, 'Even in the time of death, we would be better in our togetherness'. That was why people often went home to be with their families and neighbours.

For some young men and children, it became a sort of entertainment and they would hang about to see what was going on. The district of Kaniashqan was the first place where people expected the gunmen to arrive. Sometimes, the revolutionaries lingered there without starting to shoot government posts until late afternoon or evening. The young men, especially the newest volunteers, would walk about in their khaki peshmarga costumes, showing off with their guns. They came in broad daylight to demonstrate that they were not scared to fight for their country.

Sajid often went out early to buy fresh bread for the family. One morning, he turned at the sound of trampling footsteps. Several gunmen were running towards him, carrying two extra Kalashnikovs stained with blood. The revolutionaries were hurrying towards Kaniashqan after ambushing two Iraqi soldiers in the town centre who had been sent to buy hot food and fresh bread for their officers. For Sajid, this was not a happy way to start the day and he feared there would be more trouble in the days ahead. By the time new government divisions arrived in Halabja, the peshmargas had left for the mountains, but the Doshka long-range sub-machine guns on the T-55 tanks were shooting at the suburbs, hills and plains around Halabja before they entered the town.

A few days later, Sajid went with Hoshyiar, his neighbour's son, to get some flu medicine from the town hospital. It was a strange day for anyone to go to hospital, just after another shoot-out, with a few killed on both sides. However, children were getting used to this situation, which had become the norm.

As Sajid and Hoshyiar left the hospital, they heard the loud volley of Bren sub-machine gun fire. They turned to see a little smoke in the air and a young man, in bluish-grey traditional Kurdish costume, collapsed and bleeding on the pavement.

An army officer, revolver in his hand, walked towards him. The officer squatted down and shot the Kurd twice in the head. This was the first time Sajid had witnessed a cold-blooded murder. It was such a horrible and unforgettable scene.

Sajid and Hoshyiar turned and ran home. They told their families what they had just witnessed and later they learned the whole story. The victim's brother was a peshmarga who had been killed earlier in the day while trying to flee the town as the army forces approached with their Doshka sub-machine guns blazing. The victim had then come to Halabja from the nearby Shnrwie village to ask for his brother's corpse. It was his bad luck that a harsh new commander, Adnan Muhamed Noori, was in town. He heard about the young man's request and ordered his officers to quickly find and kill him. He was shot just across the street from the hospital. His only fault was to want a decent burial for his brother.

The young man had just finished secondary school. In one family two sons were murdered on the same day. Life in the revolution meant getting used to these killings, and the victims became like the sparrows hit by kids' catapult shots. It was so sad

that human life was becoming so cheap, although
for a victim's family, children, relatives and friends,
years of grief lay ahead.

For the ordinary person, this became the way of life.
One had to cope with it, get used to it and carry on.
Not one family that Sajid knew thought of leaving
the region in the 1960s, not even to go to other,
Arab, parts of Iraq. Halabja was their whole world,
whether or not they survived all its hardship and
grief. There was no escape and one had to get on
with life as it was. However, with no hope left, many
young men would go to the mountains to fight back.

Everyone was vulnerable and affected in some way.
There was nowhere to go. It was not easy to find a
job and accommodation if anyone wanted to go
elsewhere. Peace became priceless and hardly
anyone could afford it.

In the early years of the revolution, leaving the town
would mean being uprooted like an old tree with
long, spread-out roots. One could not simply chop
off all the roots of friendship, family, neighbourhood
and scenery, the shared anxiety and enjoyment of
social relations at mosques, tea shops, orchards,
plains, mountains and schools, the little chats and
jokes at the shops and listening to gossip. It was
never easy for anyone to turn their back on all that
and leave.

During one of the army's retaliatory rampages, Sajid's family became victims of the terror. Government gunmen came down through the alleyways searching for 'terrorists', as they used to call revolutionaries. A jash mercenary and an Arab police officer, his left hand bandaged and a pistol in his right hand, stormed into their house.

 'You lie down. I am going to kill you,' the policeman told Sajid's father, his Arab words being translated by the jash.

'No need to lie down now. When he kills me, I will lie down anyway,' Sajid's father told the jash to tell the policeman.

They exchanged a few words in Arabic and then the jash turned to Sajid's father and said, 'The policeman asks for money', implying that if he paid up he would be left unharmed. As he had no cash on him, Sajid's father sent his eldest son to his brother's house, a few doors down, to borrow three and a half dinars. When he handed over the money, the gunmen left. This kind of treatment angered the people of Halabja, encouraging many more young men to join the revolutionaries in the mountains.

For Sajid and the family, it was a scary incident. They had seen the police officer, with his revolver in his bare hand, threatening to kill their father. They had watched in horror and could not say anything, but it turned out that the man was simply exploiting the situation to rob people of their little savings.

Battalion 20

In July 1964, there was a big battle in the plain of Sharazour. It was one of the first head-on clashes when young men of Halabja and surrounding villages went out to fight the invading army. The freedom fighters tried to dig up the main road to Slemani in many places, to make it difficult for the army to advance. In addition, they prepared a few lines of resistance close to the main road that linked the town of Halabja to the regional city of Slemani, about 70 kilometres away.

Battalion 20, led by Zaem (Brigadier) Sadiq, an Arab officer from the Mosul area, was approaching with three to four thousand soldiers, accompanied by 36 T-55 tanks and more than 100 jash mercenaries. The peshmarga forces had informers in Sharazour town, where the army gathered for their campaign to go through the Sharazour plain towards Halabja. The Kurdish forces were as yet novices in fighting a guerrilla war, and lacked the necessary weapons. Their forces amounted to between 50 and 70 gunmen. However, despite their small numbers, for about a week they confronted the mighty Battalion 20, and slowed its advance on Halabja.

Despite the flatness of the landscape, which was a few kilometres away from the mountains, the revolutionaries used the roadside marshland, thickets and bushes as cover. About 30 of their gunmen were positioned quite close to the main road, to shoot at the tanks and army vehicles on their way. There were groups of armoured vehicles, followed by soldiers and jash on a slow march by foot.

The peshmarga, who were well hidden in the thickets and marshland, started shooting at the armoured vehicles and the infantry, while further back a few snipers targeted the drivers of the tanks and armoured vehicles.

In their first attempt, lasting a few hours, 15 to 20 of the military were killed or wounded. No one could go close enough to check, because the tanks and armoured vehicles retreated from the scene to a safer place where an ambulance could pick up the casualties

A few days later, the army tried again, as though testing the guerrillas' resistance. The second time, they came with a larger force. This time the peshmarga forces had a sub-machine gun set up on one of the hills near the Zalm bridge.*

* Zalm is a small river that comes down from the mountain waterfall of the holiday resort of Ahmad Awa, about 10 km away in the Hawraman/Zagros Mountains. The river joins Lake Sharazour towards the Sirwan river and Derbendi Khan dam further down in the Sharazour plain.

The peshmarga forces were ready, with a sub-machine gun and homemade bombs. The peshmargas' planning and organisation had been managed by some former Iraqi army soldiers who had joined the revolutionaries on Hawraman Mountain. The resistance was effective and, once again, the army retreated back to Sharazour town.

Third time around, the peshmarga forces were better organised still, but now the government forces were greater in number and accompanied by the air force. However, the planes were ineffective because the two sides were so close to each other and they could not risk bombing their own forces. The fighting started near Zalm bridge and lasted for a few hours until the government forces withdrew. This time they had managed to kill six peshmargas and capture one man. They interrogated him without success and then tortured him to death by tying him to a tank which dragged him all the way back to Sharazour town.

The peshmarga fighters resisted for a week and many people from Halabja and surrounding villages prepared food for them, made ammunition and gave their assistance day and night. Many were in a joyful mood to be able to resist, contribute and help in whatever way possible.

In their final assault, in August 1964, the army advanced with 36 tanks and this time they made it into Halabja.

When Brigadier Sadiq led Battalion 20 in to Halabja, Sajid saw him as a short, stocky, pale-skinned, middle-aged man with soft eyes, a small nose and fat neck. He led his army with many artillery pieces: 36 T-55 tanks, many armoured vehicles and lorries with piles of sandbags stacked up on both sides. The soldiers and mercenaries were inside the trucks with holes made for them to fire their weapons.

In their final assault, they caused killing, burning and destruction in many villages. Facing overwhelmingly superior forces, the peshmargas were forced to withdraw to the mountains.

Sajid was too young to be seen as a threat, and he was too innocent to be scared. He went to Halabja's high street and counted the 36 T-55 tanks. As they passed by, he felt the ground shaking. Sajid now saw exactly what those glossy colourful posters, distributed to the people of Halabja by the communists some years before, had displayed. When the posters of Russian armoured vehicles, tanks and aeroplanes were handed out for free in Halabja, it was said that these weapons would be used against the evil forces of imperialism. In reality, however, they were being used to suppress the Kurds' demands for basic human rights and civil law.

Local people learned how cruel Brigadier Sadiq was, when his army bombed many villages across the Sharazour plain. He already had a terrible reputation. In 1963, when he failed to capture the Azmir heights overlooking the city of Slemani, his troops unleashed their rage on the civilian population. They rounded up about 180 young men and shot them dead. Brigadier Sadiq himself walked into a house and, when he saw that the family had eight boys, he took two of them away to be shot. 'That family had too many boys,' he said.

As the Kurdish forces withdrew to the mountains, the army proceeded towards Halabja. Tanks and armoured vehicles encircled the town and they bombarded the surrounding plains and mountains, firing with their crackling, heavy sub-machine guns. The hooting and swishing tank shells peppered the sky above Halabja, and all the families and children shivered with fear. They just had to wait and see. Fortunately, the shells were not aimed at Halabja's civilians, but people were still anxious that the army would come down hard on them, as so often happened.

Just before Battalion 20 arrived in Halabja, a few elderly and notable men got together, wanting to do something to persuade Brigadier Sadiq to leave the civilian population alone. They contacted him through the town's governor. The elders of the town suggested that they should go and welcome Sadiq to try and avoid any harm to the civilians.

These men took seven sheep to sacrifice before the Brigadier, as a symbol of respect. However, the army still bombed many villages in the Sharazour plain and hills around Halabja, causing several casualties. Halabja was safe for the time being, but many villagers were killed or wounded. Their harvests and dry pastures caught fire and burned. There was smoke everywhere, and many areas of the mountain slopes turned black from the fires.

While Battalion 20 and the jash gunmen were in Halabja, the peshmarga forces could no longer come to town during the day. However, when night fell, they would return to attack government posts in the north of the town, next to the main hospital and near to the Mier Garden, the 'Baghi Mier'.

These attacks happened quite often, and the peshmarga used the Mier orchard and adjacent Mordana, a place of tree shrubs, to attack government forces. Soon Brigadier Sadiq ordered his troops to destroy the orchard and uproot all the trees. The presence of Brigadier Sadiq in Halabja signalled the end forever of the Mier Garden and its famous merry evenings.

In the following years, all the town's other orchards were destroyed and uprooted. The climate became drier, hotter and more barren with many animals, birds and butterflies left without habitats to survive.

Brigadier Sadiq's Battalion 20 began attacking the peshmarga forces, but the mountainous terrain was not easy for their manoeuvres. The main headquarters of the peshmargas were in the villages of Biyara and in Taweila, further up in the Hawraman Mountains.

Biyara was closer. When the army marched towards the village, it met such a fierce resistance that it was forced to retreat. This was one of the first big confidence boosts for the revolutionaries.

The army did not stay long in Halabja, pulling out after a few weeks. The government sent in tribal

Arabs from the South as police recruits. Because the newcomers did not speak the local language, they were useless as policemen, though they provided a bit of extra trade for the local shopkeepers.

The revolution was still in its early years, and a few of the revolutionaries, known for their bravery and key role in operations, became more powerful. There was a problem when the ones who were not well educated and sometimes even illiterate became empowered by their success. The new illiterate revolutionaries created some problems for the cause because they were asking local people for money and weapons in the name of the revolution. They especially made demands on the tribal leaders who were relatively wealthy. This led to many grave mistakes when they used force against their own people to get guns, money and, sometimes, women.

Even before Battalion 20 arrived, there was trouble involving some of the up-and-coming young gunmen. They had never enjoyed any position of authority, power and money. Some of them were jealous of those old veterans, landowners and tribal leaders who did, such as one tribal leader who was well known and respected as a revolutionary and who owned plots of land, cattle, horses, a divan and guns. This was the man Sajid and his friends had been thrilled to watch as the leading horseman during the '12 Cavaliers of Marivan' display in the Newroz celebrations following the fall of the monarchy.

When one of the illiterate revolutionaries sent some men to ask for his guns, he of course refused because this was an insult to his honour. The men were sent back and again he refused to hand over his guns. When they tried to detain him, he pulled out his pistol and killed two of the peshmargas.

A bigger force of gunmen, intent on revenge, was sent against him. The man did not want to run to the government or become a jash traitor to his country. Instead he defended himself and he was killed in a shoot-out in the orchards of his village. When one of his daughters tried to protect her dying father with her own body, she was shot and injured.

This was an example of the true spirit of sacrifice of Kurdish women who bore much of the burden of sustaining families and communities. In the Kurdish countryside, women looked after the children, farms and herds, and made fresh bread for their families three times a day. They prepared dairy products, worked in the farm and orchards and yet were still happy, loving their families and their way of life in the mountains.

The killing of the tribal leader was one of the first big mistakes made by someone from the KDP in the area. No action was taken against the culprit. The party did not seem to have an internal disciplinary system that would have led to an investigation and the questioning and punishment of someone who had clearly committed crimes of plunder and murder.

Incidents such as this created divisions among Kurds that were exploited by the government. It helped them to recruit more Kurdish mercenaries and build the jash into a significant irregular force of Kurds fighting alongside the Iraqi regime.

The regime called the peshmargas insurgents and 'mukharibeen': terrorists. The establishment of the jash enabled the government to wage a 'low intensity war', a kind of war between the people themselves, a type of hidden war for which the regime might avoid blame, while weakening the revolutionaries.

After a while, Battalion 20 left Halabja and the peshmarga forces often came to town during the day, staying, like before, from afternoon until late night or early morning while the shops remained locked up. This harmed the livelihoods of many local people who were self-employed as traders, shopkeepers or skilled artisans. Only those with a salary, such as teachers, nurses, government officials, jash, police and army personnel weren't affected.

Between 1963 and 1969 there were five regime changes, usually by coup d'état. During one of those changes, with a ceasefire and the prospect of negotiations, many revolutionaries came back to the town, and a group of seven jash gunmen came to kill one of them. While this revolutionary was standing in front of his shop, the gunmen appeared from the south end of the high street, and his friends urged him to leave.

He was gone before the gunmen reached his shop and so they went down the road, looking for his younger brother's shop. This young man was newly married and had a shoe shop. He was not involved in the revolution. He thought that he would be safe and that is why he did not leave town with his brother.

Sajid's father heard his pleas with the gunmen, as they lined up across the road from his shop, pointing their guns. 'For God's sake, don't, don't kill me!' he begged them. 'Oh, God I have nothing to do with the revolution. Take all my shop, money, whatever you want. Oh God, what have I done?'

Bang, bang, bang. They shot him many times with their MK1 guns. All of them together, they all took part in his murder. They killed him in cold blood, in the centre of the town with many witnesses. They were stood in front of Ali Salim's big tea shop in the town centre aiming their seven guns at one unarmed man in his shoe shop. All the other shopkeepers saw what was happening. 'Oh God, have mercy,' they thought. But they dared not interfere or say anything and the young man was shown no mercy.

No one from the government held any investigation, even though the murder took place during a ceasefire when incidents like that should not happen.

All the shopkeepers were upset and angry and they closed their shops for a few days in protest. It seemed as though the whole town took part in the funeral ceremony. The cemetery was located slightly out of the town, and the peshmarga brother arrived with a few other gunmen. He came to thank the shopkeepers for their solidarity. Most of the bazaar shopkeepers were mourning the shoe shop owner's death because he was their neighbour and friend.

The governor of the town and the Arab army people never questioned what had happened. In fact, the government wanted more division between Kurds and they always used the policy of divide and rule. That was one of the first incidents indicating that any hope of meaningful negotiations and a settlement was false. It wasn't long before full-scale hostilities resumed.

In the years that followed, the revolutionary took his revenge on the mercenaries. He exterminated six of them, though the seventh fled the region and was never seen again. But nothing would bring his brother back to life.

In Halabja, as in many Kurdish towns and cities, the bazaar became an arena for violence, with clashes between peshmargas and the army and jash forces or even between rival Kurdish nationalist factions. Quite often, passers-by were wounded, disabled or killed.

When this fighting was between Kurds, it was as though it had nothing to do with the government. This was the low intensity warfare in operation and it helped pave the way for the policy of genocide, or race killing, by the regime.4.

1.   (Robben and Nordstrom 1995, 1, 3) Kristina Koivunun, p.57 The invisible War in North Kurdistan published by ministry of Culture KRG 1995

2. Kashkol p.45 – 58

3. The Genocide of Barzani People, 18

4. From Shnerwie to Stockholm, by Hamai Faraj, published in Slemani 2006 23, 31

5. (Klare and Kornbluh 1987, 3, 9) Kristina Koivunun, The invisible War in North Kurdistan, KRG Publication 2005 40, 41

6.   Iraq since 1958, from Revolution to Dictatorship by M. Farouk Singlett & Petaslinglett 1987

2.   The Social Life of Halabja
A.   Three Chains of Mountains

When Sajid was in secondary school, he wrote the following about Halabja:

In the mid-fifties, when the window of life was wide open before me in Halabja, I found myself on the high ground, standing before three chains of mountains. These were often the sceneries of my leisure time for many years to come. I was so attracted by their colourful views: grey, green, yellow, rusty, purple and white, with heaps of dark shadows in the evenings and nights. There was an orange ambience at dusk and bright, golden streaks of light at dawn, peering from behind rocky ridges and peaks, followed by glaring sunshine with the midday summer heat.

When I was out in the surrounding plains, alone and always looking up, for years and years I wanted to look into their folds to explore: so many creases, shrubs and woods as if hidden from me, so much to see. I often imagined their past: for so many hundreds of years, for so many generations, they were our little world's frontiers. We lived with their changing panoramas, differing shades, tones, colours and moods in four seasons.

This was in parallel with the changing moods and stages of my growing up, until I left Halabja unexpectedly some years later.

For so many years, they have been standing before us, aloof and defiant in their enormity, and it was as though we were looking at each other in silence. It seemed that we would never get tired of each other's company. The only difference was that we were temporary inhabitants and they were the permanent lords of the land. I sometimes thought, 'If only they could tell me what they have witnessed in the past hundreds of years, it would be fascinating. Oh, I pray to God, if only one day they would start to tell me about that.

There was a saying that, 'Every Castle has a story to tell' and one may consider that every bit of these mountains may have their own narratives. Throughout their past – from the Gooties and Parikani, from the Assyrians' Zamwa to the Medes and Sassanid – these mountains have witnessed the passing of many different communities, and many little villages and towns like Halabja.

Taking into account the rich history of the area, every yard of the area must have seen events: battles, encounters, many scenes of happiness or grief that never have been perceived by others. Some people's experience of being away for years would make them understand the extent of loving one's own land, appreciating from far away that there is such a strong bond to one's native place.

What is it in that place that has enchanted me so much, and proved worthy of people giving sacrifice for her protection? Here is the cosy haven of orchards, mountains and plains and the harmonious relations flowing from the simplicity and contentment of the lives of people who were happy with whatever little they had.

People always wanted to be free as air. They often got together, as if hugged in the arms of these mountains and orchards, and were always longing to meet up for a national or religious celebration or ceremony, or simply for a chat, tease, laugh and to freely shout at the top of their voices. This was how the scenery won their affection.

In this simple and innocent way of life, people so easily won others' affection and just a 'Salaam' could be enough to make a friend. It was not only the beauty and mystery of the views that made one love the mountains, but also the way life was shaped within their folds for many years.

One would clearly see people's dejection after a social meeting when they said farewell to each other. That feeling of togetherness had been formed over many years. That was why it was not easy to abandon Halabja, despite the fear of being shot dead or blown apart. That was why, when someone died, everyone was ready to help with the burial ceremony and, when someone was poor, many assisted with food and anything they could.

If only these people had been left alone and allowed to get on with their chosen way of life. Whatever we had would have been enough, because our mountains, plains, springs and streams would supply us with nourishment. Oh, the whiff of narcissus in spring, the glow of tender petals of red poppy flowers, the many colourful wild flowers and roses, the orchards and cherry trees' pink and white blossoms, the sweet and colourful fruits of mulberry in the hills and plains in late spring, the mountains' oak, the acacia and other shrubs - they were like a heaven to one's eyes in the misty air.

There was the colourfulness of the shops' vegetables and fruits, with the perfume of narcissus, roses and violet flowers. The smell and spectacle of mellow fruits in summer and early autumn, the various banquets of traditional food, the traditional dance, poetry and folk songs. The merry evenings at Gulan and the Mier Garden, and the children's summer nights: gathering at someone's door around a lamp post and singing, giggling and playing chawsharkie (hide and seek) until late, when everyone had had enough and went home into the silence of the night.

The underlying reason for one's admiration was the town's innocent and simplistic social relations, the careful consideration of its neighbourhood calm and the peaceful atmosphere reigning over its residences, the love and respect for Halabja, the homeland for my heart, and the years of teenage love. That was why Halabja, between these enormous mountains, was like a paradise. As in ancient history, these mountains were revered like Divine providence. That was why, for hundreds of years, the mountains have been looked up to as Kurds' only friends.

B. Baghi Mier, (The Prince's Garden)

In the early 1950s there was a vibrant social life in Halabja. Half the town was covered with trees and orchards, and there so many water springs in many places. To the west is the Kaniashqan district, going down into a valley that opens up to the west end of the town. One of the best-known places there was Baghi Mier (the Prince's Garden) and next to it was the Mordana area of berry bushes, one of the well-known place for evening walk after dinner.

Baghi Mier had a water spring and many orchard trees such as pomegranates, figs, vines, plums and apple trees. There were also tall, slim cypresses, and many mulberry trees, plots of various types of vegetables, all fenced with blackberry bushes and other bushes and shrubs.

In summer evenings, Baghi Mier was always vibrant with noise. It was where so many young and middle-aged men gathered. It sounded as though there was an endless party going on. By the water spring there was a gazebo with many chairs. On a small mud-brick bench there was a tea set, and next to it, the barbecue set which looked as though it had been in use for generations, where a few men were making kebabs. A few more were on the far side, preparing salads and other side dishes. At the barbecue they grilled sheep entrails, lamb meat and chicken. There were various types of alcoholic drinks available: 'Araq' Ouzo, whisky, beer and wine. In addition, there was yoghurt, green salads, boiled chickpeas, salted nuts, pickles, sultanas, sherbet and soft drinks.

The gatherings carried on until late night or early morning. Many gambled as they played backgammon and dominos. Men often came from the regional city of Slemani and from other surrounding towns and villages. Baghi Mier was famous all over Kurdistan for its merry summer evenings.

Anyone who came to this place for the first time would see, hand in hand, mulberry, apple, pear and fig trees, swaying in the evening breeze, as though dancing to the folk music of Baghi Mier. In this merry mood, there was no space left for sorrow. People came to have fun, play dominos, have a drink and listen to music. Some joined in the singing and they would not care what might happen the next day.

The atmosphere was always welcoming. On the other side, the master kebab maker, Asaadi Kebabchi, was busy, covered in the lingering fog of smoke from grilling shish kebabs on the barbecue set. Every now and then, sparks of fire darted at his face but he did not care and sniffed and wiped his eyes. He kept greeting his steady flow of customers with a smile. A few were still in the mood to complete jokes from the evening before. This was clear when someone raised his hand and protested, 'No please, kaka giyan (dear brother), leave that one for later or tomorrow', as though the drink had not reached his head yet and it would take some time to get in the mood to carry on joking and teasing. A bit further away, a few more people banged their open hands together in greeting and, with a considerable measure of friendship and pleasure, put their right hands across their chests to express their feelings.

On the other side of the spring was an arrangement of flat stones like small. cobbled squares for people to sit and wash or relax beside the refreshing crystal-cool water. There was a group by the side of the spring and the sound of laughter went up and down, with people raising their heads and arching their backs to release their loud laughs to the skies. Others joined in with smiles to share in the joy of the joke.

Further along, another group was playing backgammon, throwing their dice as their arms jolted automatically up and down. They seemed tense and there were some loud protests: 'No! Do not catch the dice, let us play fair, no cheating, it is not right.'

They played music, joked, laughed, and sang until late night or early morning. A few of the well-known local singers often performed. Later, as they headed back to their homes, they merrily sang along the roads and alleyways.

Kurds love music and are fond of storytelling and reciting poems. There are many lyrics and poems about the beauty of Kurdistan and Kurdish women. There are many poems and lyrics about Kurdish heroes, both ancient and modern.

That was how they lived. Culture, nature and nurture was the tripod that created the framework of their imagination. They based their approach to life on the innocence and simplicity of nature, wanting to live for the day and not worry about what the next day would bring.

These places of merry evenings divided the local people, as the fun-loving folks visited the orchards of Baghi Mier, Mordana, and the valley of Gulan while devout religious people never joined them and were instead at the convents and mosques. However, even if they wanted to, they lacked the power to stop the merriment.

In winter, the Baghi Mier people went to 'Nadi Muwazafin', the officers' club next to the governor's office, near the town's main hospital. The men gathered there and carried on drinking and playing until late night or early morning. These gatherings were always just for men. There was not a single woman who could share in these vibrant evenings for religious reasons because the segregation of men and women was a part of the Islamic cultural tradition.

C. The Ahmedawa Holiday Resort

The Ahmadawa holiday resort near Halabja in the Surein Mountain, in the southern part of the Hawraman mountain range, was always crowded during spring and summer weekends. Many families headed there from all over the country. Ahmadawa is about 20 miles from Halabja, and five miles from the Zalm Bridge in the Sharzour Plain. It is deep within a Y-shaped rocky gorge before the peaks of Surein, the grey-purple mountain rocks towering above Halabja and the Sharzour Plain. Ahmadawa is known for its beautiful waterfall, flowing from high up in the mountain and cascading down to a rocky stream covered from both sides by thickets, shrubs and orchard trees for more than a mile. It streams down towards the Sharzour Plain through the little town of Khormal at the foot of the mountain.

From 1970 to 1974, when there was no threat of army clashes, people were happy and hopeful that the 1970 11the March / Azar agreement would be implemented and create a lasting peace. In 1973, Sajid accompanied a few family guests, from Baghdad and the city of Slemani, to Ahmadawa where they stayed for a few days. This armistice period was one of the most pleasant of times, when people were free from fear.

The sun slipped down behind the huge rocks of the Ahmadawa valley and a dark shadow seemed to bring on the evening sooner than anywhere else in the world. Many families had come for a few days' holiday and each had hired a pitch in the valley's orchard. They prepared traditional foods, especially barbecued shish kebabs and various fruits and delicacies. The visitors made temporary shacks beside the cascading river, where they left drinks and fruit to cool in the freezing stream.

For Sajid and his guests, this was an exciting night they would never forget. In the middle of the summer the temperature was above 40 degrees Celsius in other parts of the country, but deep in the orchard valley of Ahmadawa it stayed so beautiful, refreshing and cool.

The cascading river provided rhythmic, orchestral night-time music and, in the morning, they awoke to multifarious bird songs. Although this place offered respite from the scorching summer, no one stayed idle during the day. Instead they went climbing up and down the mountain rocks and explored the surrounding gorges, thickets and ravines.

It was also a chance to switch off and relax, listen to music, or play backgammon or dominos to pass the time. One had to watch out for the kids who were fascinated by the mesmerising atmosphere and might wander too deep into the rocky valley under so many orchard trees and bushes. Without the fear of war and revolution, the country's mountainous

It was unfortunate that the regime had never been serious about the 1970 ceasefire, and scarcely two years passed before its true intentions became known. The Iraqi regime's cynical hope was that the two heavily armed Kurd groups would clash and cause a flood of Kurdish blood. However, the two leaderships held talks and agreed to reunite.

D. The Halabja Air attack with TNT bombs 26th April 1974

It was an example of the crimes against humanity, the crimes of genocide committed by the Iraqi Ba'athist regime, when it deliberately bombed Kurdish civilians twice within three days. Four French-made Iraqi Sukhoi jets came to bomb Halabja in the mid-afternoon of 26 April. People were already expecting them because they had bombed the town of Qaladzyia, 100 miles away, on 24 April and killed about 180 civilians. Many had fled Halabja when they got this news, but others stayed behind, including young volunteers who wanted to assist in the self-defence and to help with casualties.

These volunteers dug holes in the ground and prepared bomb shelters. One of the biggest bombs was a TNT bomb hit the middle of the bazaar, creating a three by four-metre hole and bursting the town's main water pipe. All the surrounding shops collapsed and caught fire and 63 civilians, shopkeepers and passers-by were killed or mutilated, and many were wounded.

Sajid's brother Ali witnessed the bombing and this is his story.

'I went to the sweetshop with a banknote to get some change. I looked out and saw my father across the street, standing in front of his shop. A few minutes later I heard the siren when I was about a hundred yards north of where the TNT bomb dropped in the town centre.

'I was desperate to find shelter and went into a small shop where I hid under a metal table. A huge explosion shook everywhere so violently that the shop's aluminium shutters shattered and pieces of metal flew about the place. The metal table saved me. Many other shops were closed, and their shutters were hurled out as if they were all open.

'A few minutes after the bombing I came out into the street and saw that peshmarga fighters were there helping the victims. I saw two of my cousins nearby. I was very worried about my family, and so I hurried home to find out if they were all right. Then I started looking for my father.

'On my way I saw that many doors and windows of shops and houses had been thrown wide open by the explosion. I saw a young man's body. His back was badly wounded, and the flow of blood from his wounds was subsiding. He was one of my friends. It was the first time I had seen the town in such a horrific state.

'There was such a terrifying silence. I started shouting at the top of my voice, desperate to hear someone. No one from among my relatives, family and neighbours replied, and still I was desperately shouting like mad. People were so shocked that no one would utter a word. I headed towards the mosque with an unconscious willingness in my pace, as if I was leaping forward with desperate steps, looking for my father. I met one of my neighbour's sons.

"No, I haven't seen him," the young man said.

'I turned and ran towards my father's shop. I looked at the sweetshop where I had gone to get some change minutes before the bombing. It had collapsed and nearby there was the body of a ten-year-old boy, the son of my father's friend. I felt his body. It was still warm. I checked his pulse for any sign of life, but there was none.

'He was that family's only son. His father too was murdered in the bombing. A young innocent child was killed because of his race. They did not let him live more than 10 years. At that tender age he was blown apart by the fascist Ba'athist's bomb. Nearby, there was a big hole from the TNT explosive that had landed in the middle of adjoining streets, causing most of the fire, destruction and death.

'Water from the burst pipe had created a big pond. Survivors were working to put out fires, collect corpses – there were about 20 bodies near the centre of the blast and more elsewhere – and take the injured to the local hospital. My father's shop had been burned to the ground but there was no sign of him anywhere. "They took several bodies to the mosque," a young man told me.

'They were taking corpses to all the town's mosques and I went around them, checking the clothes of victims whose bodies were about to be taken to the graveyard. But I did not find my father. I kept going, checking all Halabja's mosques. They were overwhelmed with corpses. When I heard that some bodies had been taken to mosques in Sirwan village, I began that 11-kilometre journey but soon came across my sisters and my brother coming back from the village. They assured me that our father was not there.

'We spent the night with no news of him and, early in the morning, we started looking for him again, with a few relatives and friends who came to help us. We searched among the debris of the collapsed shops and buildings but still found no trace of him.

'The next night we all felt desperate. One of my sisters woke us up early, crying about her dream. "I saw father," she said. "He told me, 'Come, I am here, you can find me here.'"

"I know where he is," she kept saying. "Wake up, let's go. I know where he is."

'Across the road from father's shop, and close to the TNT bomb site, a two-storey building behind the sweetshop had collapsed and we started lifting its debris. Then we found him. His body was all crushed, flattened almost like a piece of paper.

'It was such a terrible spectacle. No one would ever wish to see their father like this. It was so horrific. The scene would never leave our memories. This was what Arab Muslim brothers did to Kurds.

'With the help of neighbours, relatives and friends, we moved the debris and collected father's remains. These were not even in the shape of a human body.

We collected his remains in a sack and took them to the mosque. The agony of trying to find him had been replaced by the certainty of grief. Our father had nothing to do with the politics of the revolution. He was about 60 years old and one of 63 people killed in the bombing, with more than a hundred injured.'

That was an episode in the life of revolution in Halabja. At the time, almost no one knew that there were much worse to come. Many naively thought that this was the ultimate grief and distress.

The revolutionaries had trained their anti-air force guns on the four French- made Iraqi fighter jets, especially the gunner on the fourth floor of the 'Tankih Tobacco' building who kept firing with a sub-machine gun. But it was obviously not enough to deter the planes from dropping TNT bombs on the civilian population in the high street. This was the centre of the town, where many shops and the bazaar were situated. Targeting a civilian population certainly amounted to the crime of genocide – just like two days before, when they killed about 200 civilians, mainly college and university students, in the town of Qaladiza.

But the bombing failed to destroy the revolution. Instead it added more sore wounds to the determination of the revolutionaries, making them fight harder than ever before.

1. The Road Less Travelled, by M Scott Pek 1978.108–109

2. 'Benjamin Franklin was one of the Founding Fathers of the United States. A noted polymath, Franklin was a leading author, printer, political theorist, politician, postmaster, scientist, musician, and inventor.'

3. The Road Less Travelled, M Scott Peck p; 256

4. IBID P.156–157

5. The Road Less travelled, M. Scott Peck, 161–165

6. Richard Swinburne, professor of philosophy of Christian Religion at Oxford University, England. 'What

 Philosophers Think, edited by Julian Baggani & Jeremy Stangmoor 2003 p. 105–113'

7. The Road Less Travelled, M. Scott Pek p.179

8. Don Cupitt, religion & Ethics, borne in Lancashire, Trinity Hall Cambridge, see Don Cupitt.

 9. Frantz Omar Fanon (20 July 1925– December 1961)

10. (Munts book) M Scott, The Road Less Travelled, 1978 45, 47

11. Erich Fomm from the, Road Less Travelled M. Scott Pek 1978 72

12. Christopher Hitchens the Trial of Henry Kissinger, Printed in Great Britain Atlantic Books 2002, 192, 193

E.   The Bombing of the District of Kaniashqan, 13th May, 1987

Halabja was always in the frontline of the Iraqi Kurdish uprising. It was once again, on 13th May 1987, when the regime started a campaign of mass relocation and destruction of many villages around the town. The people of Halabja wanted to resist and there was an announcement by loudspeakers from the mosques, calling on people to gather for a demonstration. Many responded, and the protests spread to the villages of Sirwan and the wider area around Halabja, all calling for the regime to stop the destruction of Kurdish villages. The Iraqi regime was implementing its Anfal campaign of genocide against Kurds by destroying their villages and relocating the villagers to concentration camps.

The regime's soldiers and Mukhabarat agents responded to the peaceful protests with bullets. The first victim was a young man called Mariwan and many others were injured. The killing angered the people even more and, after three days of demonstrations, the regime called in helicopter gunships to bomb the district of Kani-Ashqan.

This bombing killed 22 people and injured about 50, mostly civilians, including Hama Faraj Abdulla, Sajid's friend, and his uncle Osman Hadji Salih.

When the peshmargas withdrew from the area, the wounded were taken to the local hospital. However, instead of being treated, under the cover of darkness they were buried alive, along with several of those already killed. It was not until the next day that people discovered that government forces had buried them all in a mass grave near the village of Bamouk, about a mile outside the town. There was already a genocide campaign in progress, and the regime's aggressive response was intended to terrify the people and prevent the demonstrations from spreading to other parts of Kurdistan. 1

1. Hashtaw Hasht, the Kurdish Magazine, Spring & Summer 2006 75 -77

F. The Chemical Attack on Halabja Civilians, 16th March, 1988

Halabja was one of the main centres of the Kurdish Revolution and the cultural hub of Kurdish art, poetry and music. That was why the regime held a grudge against Halabja and ultimately tried to destroy it.

On 16th March 1988, Saddam's regime used Weapons of Mass Destruction (WMD) on a wide scale, while the whole world was watching. It was not a secret that Saddam had often used chemical weapons against Iranian forces during the eight-year long war with Iran. The Iraqi army marched deep into Iran, and the International community never considered this to be an illegal war. The Iraqi army destroyed anyone or anything in its path. They killed, plundered and destroyed all means of civilisation, while the UN and the world watched them.

When Olof Palme, the Swedish political leader, tried to bring Iran and Iraq to the negotiating table, he was assassinated. For the superpowers, the war was an opportunity to strip oil-rich Middle East countries of their hard cash assets. The war caused a destruction of both the Iraqi and Iranian economies, which served the interests of those worried that Khomeni's regime planned to attack all the Gulf countries, including Iraq, and establish its Shiite empire.

It was widely alleged that the Iranian forces, who were at the time occupying Halabja, did not allow civilians leave the town right up until the day of the chemical attack on 16th March. Iran was the first country that flew in to help the victims, and it brought in the world media to film the consequences of the attack. It is also a fact that Iran sheltered thousands of Halabja people when they crossed the border and the Iranians provided a route for humanitarian organisations to assist the victims.

It is a well-known that around 5,000 civilians were murdered and 10,000 immediately injured by the attack. In the following years, many of the injured died and, over thirty years later, they are still dying from the effects of the chemicals. It is a known fact that Saddam's regime used chemical weapons to attack Kurdish Peshmarga forces on 16th April 1987 in the Ballisan region of Kurdistan. He repeated this almost a year later in Halabja and many animals, birds and humans died instantly.

The effects of the chemical attack were so horrific. Today many of the surviving victims are disabled and infants are born dead or with deformities and fatal diseases caused by the chemicals. It seems that the suffering of Halabja must continue.

Rauf's uncle Mohamed was an eye-witness to the attack. He worked with the peshmargas as a radio operator based at Kani Gueiz, high in the Shnerwie mountain, overlooking the town of Halabja. This is his story of the chemical attack:

"As I was with the radio unit, we had to stay far behind. We were in touch with our forces in and around Halabja, to provide support and to coordinate our operations with the Iranian forces. I spoke fluent Persian.

"The Iranian attack started from the Hawraman mountain range on the right, down to Sharazour plain, and along the Zalim river which separated the two opposing sides of Iraqi and Iranian forces. About a battalion of Iraqi forces were still in Halabja but they seemed to have been cut off, with a line of Iranian forces attacking them from across the Sharzour plain along the Zalim River from the East towards the West side of the plain. Down In Halabja, the Iraqi army barracks was under continuous bombing. The Iraqi forces in Halabja had no choice but to surrender. It was also obvious that many civilians were caught up in the Iranian bombing of the Iraqi army positions in Halabja.

"On 16th March, it was only five days before Nawroz, the Kurdish New Year celebrations, and once again people in Halabja were worried about what was happening, with thousands of civilians caught between the opposing forces.

"It was a strange situation. Instead of getting ready for the Nawroz celebration, people were anxious. They knew Saddam's aeroplanes were above Tehran, the capital of Iran, and the holy city of Qum. "How can the Iranian forces defend the skies of Halabja?" local people often asked themselves. It was obvious they couldn't, and everyone knew this. The Iranian forces that occupied Halabja claimed that Saddam's regime was finished: it was not occupied anymore, and Halabja was free. "What is the point of leaving Halabja?" they said. "Halabja is free now, why should you leave?" People were not convinced, so most of people had to stay, as they were not allowed to leave.

"I saw groups of Iranian Islamic guards and other soldiers coming with big cameras with huge lenses. It was strange, as if they were getting ready to film a movie.

"We watched in horror what was happening on 16th March 1988 when, from about 11.30am, the Iraqi air force filled the sky and pounded Halabja with heavy bombing. The planes scurried around without little fear of air defences. The heavy bombing continued until about 14.30 to force all the population into underground shelters. Many houses had a shelter because Halabja had become used to bombing since the revolution started in September 1961.

"Iraq's Russian and French-made aeroplanes came in waves of groups of seven, every ten minutes. They covered the sky and bombed Halabja continuously until 14.30, and then the chemical attack started. The sound of big explosions was replaced by the quieter thuds of chemical bombs".

Saddam's regime used all kinds of banned WMD bombs in Halabja and other parts of Kurdistan. It seemed as though Saddam had a free rein to do whatever he wanted, against all principles of human civilisation.

It seemed that the purpose of the heavy bombing was to drive people into their shelters and basements. Then the chemical attack started with the fatal smell of rotten apples, bananas and other fruit discharged into the air, killing all living beings. The bombs' deadly dust rapidly spread in the air and then descended below ground into the shelters and basements.

Immediately there were casualties and many people panicked and tried to leave the town in all directions. They were desperate to escape, mainly to the North and North East of the town, on foot, in tractors, cars or whatever means of transport was available to carry families with young children, women and elderly.

As they got ready to leave, many inhaled the fatal dust of cyanide, sarin and nerve gas and other chemical substances. Many were dying on their way to safety: a few made it, but many did not. People vomited and collapsed, they screamed for help but to no avail. The alleys, roads and streets were scattered with the bodies of the dead and dying in the aftermath of the chemical attack.

Families headed towards Anab village in the hope of reaching the safety of the Hawraman Mountains. For so many it was a hopeless attempt. The aeroplanes followed them, chasing the people to slaughter them without mercy. These pilots and those who sent them had no human hearts, as they clearly knew these were families with children, desperate to reach safety. It was obvious the crowds were trying to flee the scenes of mass slaughter.

Sajid's friend Jamal tried to help his family and neighbours, holding a wet cloth to his face in an attempt to ward off the effects of the chemicals, he died on the way trying to save his family and himself.

As the radio unit watched from the 'Kani Gueiz' the Walnut Spring base, they saw aeroplanes flying so low with no fear of air defences, because there were none. Regular lines of Iraqi planes were dropping chemical bombs on the town. Jamal was one of the men who had faith in his own ability to help as many as he could. These townspeople had mostly played no part in the politics of revolution or the Iran-Iraq war. They just had the misfortune to be there.

When the bombing started, for the poor civilians it was an apocalyptic day, the end of life for many. Some mothers even threw their infants and toddlers away into rivers in the mountains- some already dead but many were still alive. Some people had nothing left but a final desperate mission for their own survival.

The scenes were incredible. Was it a dream or reality? Without the film of the Iranian camera operators, who were already nearby, it would be hard to believe it. The BBC arrived the next day to see thousands of corpses scattered everywhere in the streets and houses of Halabja. Many of the dead had burns scars, with faces darkened from the effects of the nerve gas. Many were lying facing the sky as though expecting God's mercy. They had been desperate for the international community to come to their rescue. They knew they had no part in this war and revolution. It was the graphic scene of a genocide attack in progress.

It was a terrible day. No other civilians had experienced such a horrific attack in the late twentieth century. Some were vomiting, some were laughing like mad, and some were already dead with blackened and sallow faces. Children' faces were turned into those of 90-year olds. Victims screamed in agonies of death or whined for help, but there was no one to help them. It was like how a sura of the Quran describes the apocalyptic day:

'yiawma yafir u al mareu min akhihi wa umihi wa abihi wa sahibatihi wa banihi, lekul limri ein minhum yawma ezin shaenwn yoghnihi.' This translates as: 'That is the day when one runs away from his brother, his mother, his father and from his own guardian, as everyone on the day has their own destiny to face.'

Muhamed, the radioman with the Kurdish revolutionaries, high in Kani Guiez,'the walnut spring', in the Shnrwie Mountain saw that, "all the Halabja sky was covered with dust and smoke, and there was all confusion until the night fell. Then, at about 10 pm, the aeroplanes released something like red ball cluster bombs all over Halabja and the surrounding plains, as though they were going to burn the whole area. The town looked like it was being turned to a hellfire. 'Oh God, where is God?' someone shouted'.

"The day after, when we went down to check, many of these bombs had not exploded and were stuck in the soft ploughed fields. I think it was because the fields were being prepared for the sowing of the spring season, I do not know. We did not touch the bombs but left them for military experts.

Between the villages of Anab and Jalila, there is a big mass grave, I don't know of how many are there: perhaps hundreds or even thousands. It was impossible to give proper burial ceremonies, to wash the bodies and bury them properly. It was too dangerous to touch them due to the traces of the chemicals".

Everyone should have listened to what another Halabja eyewitness said:

'Even with the slightest touch of traces of WMD, your life may finish, it may kill or disable you for life. It was such a horrible way for anyone to die. What had these innocent civilian done to go through all that? 'Why should anyone get such a severe punishment for seeking to obtain basic human rights?' Omar, one of Jamal's friends, said to one of journalists later reporting the chemical attack. To speak up for the ones who cannot speak for themselves it is not courage, it is a duty.' 1

It was such a desperate situation. Hardly anyone trying to escape took any personal belongings with them. Everyone had to try to survive, but many did not make it. They did understand the severity of the situation. They did not know that anyone who inhaled the gas or who touched the dust on the injured would eventually die or at least be blinded, disabled and mentally scarred forever. Those who experienced that horrific attack would never lead a normal life again.

This victimisation was not only for those murdered or disabled but for the whole community, and even for hundreds of innocent infants who were not yet born. It was so bizarre that millions in the West came out on protests, effectively to support Saddam's regime, when the allied forces were getting ready to topple him in 2003. Whatever has happened since the downfall of Saddam was due to Saddam's regime, which left behind it hatred, immorality, nepotism, cronyism, racism, fascism, destruction and a legacy of grief with millions dead, disabled and orphaned.

The victims were not just 5,000 or 10,000: the whole area of Halabja and Sharazour was affected and perhaps more than 100,000 people were victims.

Not only those killed or injured were victims: there were also the relatives, neighbours and friends who would suffer mental scars for life.

What happened in Halabja was not an accident of war. It was a planned genocide campaign perpetrated under the cover of the Iran-Iraq war. It was a deliberate mass race killing, and its scars will not heal for generations.

The scenes of this horror show were on world TV for about a week. They had a huge emotional impact on all Kurds and on anyone with true human feelings: perhaps the whole world was moved. However, it was obvious who had a hand in Saddam's crime of genocide, since no superpower immediately condemned the Iraqi regime, not until they were pressured by human rights organisations. Who can forget the appalling stance of the Soviet Foreign minister Eduard Shevardnadze who denied that Saddam had used chemical weapons in Halabja? While the Western media at least broadcast what had happened, the Soviet press was silent.

It was a terrible episode. Kurds had never threatened anyone's peace and security. What happened in Halabja opened windows on many aspects of human civilisation. It was so ironic and shameful that the UN, Arab League, League of Non-Aligned Nations, African League of Nations and

Islamic League of Nations did not condemn Saddam's regime immediately. In 1990, however, the international community for its own reasons quickly came to the aid of Kuwait.

 What happened in Halabja showed clearly the true faces of those nations, governments and some so-called humanitarian bodies that turned a blind eye and ignored the suffering of the victims of Anfal and the Halabja chemical attack. They abandoned Kurds to mass slaughter.

1.Hashtaw Hasht, Kurdish Magazine, June & July 2006 22 -23

2. Mohamed the Radio man from Shnerwie mountain watching what happened in Halabja

Some Eye-Witness Accounts of What Happened in Halabja

Mr Abd al Rahman lost many family members and other relatives in the Halabja chemical attack. In a 2004 interview with 'Klil' ,a Kurdish magazine, he said:

"A few days before the bombing, many people were worried, discussing and exchanging views about what they expected to happen and they were getting ready to leave the town. They kept talking about what to do, and where to go in order to avoid the inevitable chemical attack.

 "My family, my brother's family, many family relations and friends all gathered to exchange views about what to do, and where to go... We all knew Saddam was going to use chemical weapons; it was obvious Saddam had used them many times before on both civilians and in the war against Iran. About 47 members of my family and family relations were caught up in the attack, as they were trying to shelter in the basement of my brothers' house on the Western side of Kani-Ashqan district. The aeroplane spotted them and followed them with a nerve gas bomb, and no one escaped. This group of people included my brother's family and children, and my nephew who was newly married.

"It is not something we try to forget it. It is with us in our memories every day of our lives. They were all buried in a mass grave with many others, in a hurry; there was no time for any burial ceremony. One of my cousins who got caught in the attack was blinded, no one cared about him, and he has lived on the family and community's charity ever since.

"Many more victims, who were affected but survived the attack, were left with various symptoms like asthma, heart problems, shortness of breath, itchy rush, facial burns, body burns. Babies were born with deformities, and many were born dead.

 "After the chemical attack, many people escaped across the Iranian border, some of whom were injured, and others survived. After a while, many had a difficult time in Iran, as some elements of the Iranian regime put them under pressure to leave and go home, with allegations that they belonged to the Wahabi sect of Islam.

"We had no idea what Wahabi meant, although a few of our religious leaders tried secretly to help us, and brought us some medication. But it was not easy, we were continually watched and spied on and harassed by the regime. There were a few international charity organisations trying to help, but again the Kurdish internal conflict between different political parties was another obstacle before us.

Through some international organisations, a number of orphan kids were taken to Qatar, but none of the Arab countries were helpful. The charity organisations that assessed our needs always tried to help individuals and families according to the level of their desperate needs. For many of us, there was hardly anyone who would help the Halabja people; we were waiting for God's help". 1

The victims of the chemical attack and their relatives often held demonstrations in front of the German Embassy in Tehran. They knew the WMD technology had been given to Saddam's regime by German companies. Halabja people in Iran often came together from several refugee camps in Rwansar, Kameran, and Saryias to organise pickets and demonstrations against the German government and German companies.

Some who were given shelter by the Iranian regime were forced to go back into the poisoned Halabja area. They thought there was an amnesty granted by the Iraqi regime but, by the time they arrived, it had expired. About 60 Halabja families who arrived two days too late were massacred in the Anfal campaign. Many were shot dead or else their limbs were tied and they were buried alive. All were civilians: men, women and children. After the downfall of Saddam, their remains were found in mass graves in the deserts of South Iraq, near the Iraqi border with Saudi Arabia and Jordan.

1. Mr Abd Al Rahman was interviewed by the Klil Kurdish Magazine in February 2004 in Halabja

Kamaran Nawrose's Story

Kamaran Nawrose, an 11-year old boy, was the only survivor in a family of eight. His father was a friend of Sajid's elder brother: Kamaran was badly injured and picked up by an Iranian medical team three days after the attack. He needed many months of treatment. This is his story:

"I was a child, the only survivor from my family after the chemical attack on Halabja on 16th March 1988. I witnessed many died after Saddam's air-force pounded Halabja with various types of bombardment, from 11.30 am to 10 pm.

"14th March 1988 was the last day that I was able to lead a normal life with my family. We had no idea that it was to be the very last normal day for our family. There was my mum, dad, four brothers, one sister and my cousin Latif, who also lived with us. This was the day on which my whole life changed, and the last two days of my family life when I was only eleven years old.

"For us people of Halabja, the situation of war, revolution and unpredictable events had become a way of life. We had our belief in God, as it was in our religious doctrine that everyone's destiny lies in God's merciful hand. We had to surrender to God's plentiful grace and mercy. Therefore, whatever happened, whether good or bad, we could do nothing but plead for God's grace and protection. My father's day to open his teashop was his last. For me, it was my last day of attending school with my friends in primary school.

"After the sunset, once more, the wing of the darkness stretched over Halabja, and all the family was together, and life was passing as usual until midnight. We hoped and often pleaded with God to grant us another day of peace and tranquillity. We were religious, praying five times a day. We were innocent, having no part in any war or revolution. After God's grace and compassion, we had our family, neighbours and friends, and the mountains to rely on for protection. We always had belief in God, to ward off the evil of a genocide campaign against our people. We hoped God would protect us, or at least would show us a way to escape the mass slaughter of the chemical attack by the Ba'athist regime

"It was just after midnight, when the campaign of genocide turned towards Halabja. We had been through this a few times, and had run away to the mountains and sought protection, but this time, it was more scary, as we were in the middle of two armies fighting a big war. But still we could not envisage the extent of what was coming our way.

"It was after midnight and the family of Nawrose 'Chaichie' ,the teashop owner, were in bed as usual. There were several of us in a room, hoping to have a peaceful sleep until the dawn of a new day with its hope and anticipation. We heard the sound of bombing and explosions from far away.

"Because of the Iran-Iraq war, this was usual, since our town was close to the Iranian border, and the borderline had been a battlefield for the past eight years. It was another day of a war that had been going on for about eight years, we thought.

"My brothers went up to the roof of the house to check, and they came down and said, 'There seems to be a fierce fighting outside Halabja'. My father asked us to take our bedcovers and blankets down to the basement, as an initial attempt to secure our protection.

"The basement my dad had built a few months before was beneath the foreyard of the house. It was a precautionary measure for times of emergency and bombing. He built it especially for this sort of situation. The people of Halabja were accustomed to years of fighting and bombing during the revolution and the Iran-Iraq war. Many others had built similar shelters or basements for the same purpose. Ours was so strongly built and we had the belief that even TNT bombs would not destroy it. We all took our blankets and whatever we needed downstairs, and tried to sleep again.

"It sounded as though the noise of explosions was coming nearer to the town as time passed. My two elder brothers Rizgar, Rebwar and my cousin Latif climbed back onto the roof of the house, to check where the bombing was taking place. A few hours later, when dawn broke, they went out, keen to see for themselves and check the local reaction to the bombing which was getting closer to Halabja.

 "Early in the morning, there came the sound of explosions and bombing in Halabja. We saw that outside, in the alleys and streets, were groups of peshmargas. To see peshmarga forces in Halabja was never unusual. They were our men, the might of the Kurdish revolution, who often came into Halabja to do their operations against the regime's forces. They were now accompanied by other gunmen. I think they were Republican Guards or soldiers of the Islamic Republic of Iran, as they were part of the forces who had occupied or, as they termed it, 'freed' Halabja, from Saddam's despotic regime.

"They seemed to be in control of the Halabja area, from the Hawraman Mountain down to the Zalm

River and across the Sharazour plain. They said, 'Halabja is free from Saddam's regime,' but the people were not quite sure. They knew Saddam had used WMD on many occasions against Iranian forces, and against Kurdish forces in the Balisan region in 1987. They had often used WMD on the battlefields in Iran, where they managed to kill tens of thousands of Iranian republican guards and other soldiers.

"It was obvious to the local people how evil Saddam's regime was, and so they had mixed feelings when Halabja became 'free'. Their main concern was that Saddam was going to use chemical weapons against the Iranian forces in Halabja. It was obvious the fascist regime would also not hesitate to kill as many Kurds as possible.

"When the Iraqi forces in Halabja surrendered to the Iranian forces, Halabja's civilians were ready to leave the town. The presence of Iranian forces in Halabja made us more vulnerable than ever before. The Iranian forces were in control. They said, when they freed the people of Halabja from Saddam's regime, that we should stay, and they promised to protect the sky of Halabja from Saddam's air force.

"For the people of Halabja, this was a dubious claim. It was a joke: if they could not protect their own capital Teheran and Qom which were under constant bombardment by the Iraqi air force, how could they really manage to protect the Halabja sky? Therefore the civilian population was getting anxious.

"On 15th March 1988, we were passing time between happiness and anxiety as we were expecting Saddam to bomb Iranian forces in Halabja.

"My father and mother stayed at home with us, because they were worried and would not leave us. However, my two elder brothers and my cousin were always going out to find out what was happening. In the meantime, we were expecting trouble, very worried but thinking we would just have to face it. Although we knew the regime had used WMD so many times before, no one could anticipate the ferocity of Saddam's attack. It was not imaginable that we would all be targeted, including every woman and child and old person.

"We did not know when the attack would happen, and we did not know that there would be no forces there to defend the town, as the Iranians had promised. They had anti-aircraft guns and could have worn gas masks and stayed to shoot down Saddam's aeroplanes, but they did not.

"My mum prepared some food in case we needed to leave for the mountains. She boiled some eggs, prepared homemade bread, sugar, tea and cooking oil. We also got some clothes ready in case we needed to stay outside the town for longer than expected.

"The following night we stayed underground, in the basement, and a number of our neighbours joined us. Ours was one of the best bomb-shelters in the area and our numbers reached 40 in our basement of twenty square meters, We passed another night anxiously; we were all worried and hardly slept.

"The next morning, we had our sweet tea, bread and yoghurt for breakfast. As usual, my brothers and my cousin went out, but my parents stayed at home, as from experience they expected another drastic event like had happened before when we'd had to leave the town. It had happened in 1974 and in 1987 and we thought we knew how to escape and hide in the mountains.

"On 16th March 1988 at about 11am my two older brothers and my cousin were out, and my parents, sister and I were at home. When the Iraqi aeroplanes came above Halabja and started bombing, we all ran down into the bomb-shelter. A few neighbours came and, ten minutes later, my older brothers and cousin also came back down into the basement.

"The bombing continued. At the start they used heavy TNT bombs. Therefore, all the people were forced underground, into the bomb shelters. Initially they bombed the suburbs of the town, as if not to let anyone escape. This bombing continued for about three hours. They were dropping heavy bombs, every time one set of aeroplanes left, another set was ready above Halabja to continue bombing. My father thought about leaving the basement, but soon changed his mind when told that everywhere was under bombardment.

"It was dangerous to leave with all the families and children while the heavy bombing continued. It was obvious this attack would not allow civilians to leave Halabja.

"During the hours of continued heavy bombing, the noise of explosions was loud and deafening but, later in the afternoon, the noise subsided and became muffled. That was when we smelt a whiff like rotten apples, bananas or garlic. My parents soon realised that chemical weapons were being used.

"We were all very scared and panicked when chemical weapons were mentioned. Many of us were crying. We knew chemical weapons would rapidly mix with the air and eventually go down into every corner of the shelters. When that happened, the chance of escape was minimal. My mother brought a bucket of tap water with pieces of clothes and towels, to wipe and hold over our faces, to try and stop us inhaling the gas. We hoped that this would prevent or minimise injuries.

"For hours the bombing continued, and soon we felt the effects of the chemical bombing. We felt weaker, with burning sensations and our eyes watered continually. It did not take long until a chemical bomb was dropped on our next-door neighbour. This was the house of Hadji Hussein, known as Husseing Jiklet. That was when my younger brother Rebwar, who was just 10 years old, went out and climbed up onto the roof of our house to check.

"My mother called him several times, but he did not reply. Then she went after him and she took my younger brother Rizgar who was crying and clinging to her, begging her not to leave him behind. When she got to the roof top, she screamed. 'Oh God, Rebwar is dead!' When she came back down the stairs into the basement, she had already inhaled the gas with Rizgar, who she was carrying in her arms. As she was coming down, she fell. It looked as though she had tripped, but both of them died instantly. In the space of a few minutes three members of our family were dead.

"With three of us already died, everyone started screaming. Several went out of the basement, but the children stayed inside. We were told not to move at all. I stayed with my younger brother and the other children; we did not understand the severity of the situation. We stayed behind in the basement, with the instructions, 'Don't move until you are told'. I heard the voices of my dad, my sister and my brother who were crying. But later, gradually everyone went quiet until they were all silent, and none of them came back to the basement.

"The bombing continued. I sensed the smell of garlic, rotten apple and bananas. I felt very weak, my eyes watered continually. I was losing my senses, as though I was hallucinating or dreaming. I saw my mum and brother were both dead and close to me. However, I had no feeling of grief. I did not cry, I was not sad, and did not know what was happening. I was hallucinating. I was losing my strength with a burning sensation all over my body, my eyes watered, and then I felt sick and vomited I saw that all the people around me, young and old, were in agonies of death. They were dying and no one could do anything about it.

"Sometime later, in the darkness of the night, the bombing stopped and everywhere was quiet. I felt badly ill, getting weaker by the minute. I felt my face and hands were burning with blisters. There were so many blisters on my body, and everywhere was burning and painful as if I was being tortured. It was like the stories I'd heard so many times about Saddam's prisons, where they tortured prisoners to death.

"The basement now was dark, lifeless and silent. There was no voice from anyone, but sometimes I heard a very low sound of crying. I passed the night fainting and coming round and vomiting. Once, when I came round, I saw daylight outside but did not know what time it was, whether it was before midday or the afternoon. I was losing my eyesight and could hardly see.

"I was very thirsty and groped around for water. I felt the bucket which, the day before, my mum had brought. We had used it to wet clothes and towels to wet our faces for protection against the chemical poison. I wanted to drink water from it, but suddenly Hoshmand, my childhood friend and neighbour, kicked at the bucket, saying in a very low voice, 'Don't drink it, it is filthy'. Then I knew that he was alive and I did not drink it. I thought the rest of them around me were all dead, but I had lost my sense of grief, as my feelings were dead too.

"I had so much pain, and that was why I'd lost all my feelings or it was because of the chemical weapons' effects on my body. I saw that all my family, my brothers, friends and neighbours were dead, but I was not moved, and had no feeling of fear or grief.

"The next day, when a new dawn broke, I felt a bit better. I tried to get out from the basement looking for my dad and my sister. I tried to find out what had happened to my brothers. I tried to get up, but I could not at all.

"I thought I was crippled. I tried hard, using my elbows and knees. I tried to crawl over the dead bodies lying around. I tried hard until I reached the door of the basement. 'Oh God, how can I climb up the stairs?' I thought. I still managed to crawl up the stairs, up to the foreyard. It was two days since the chemical attack. After two days, for the first time, I could see the daylight. My visual sense was very weak. I hoped I could find some people who would get me away from that congregation of death in the basement. I saw the bodies of my two older brothers and my sister nearby, My brother Rebwar's head was on the lap of my sister Dilxwaz.

"My elder brother Rizgar's body was next to them. My father was farther away, in front of the bath door. My sight was very poor but I could see it was my father's body. There was blood on his body. A few people from Halabja later told me what had happened. They saw my father in the last few minutes of his life. 'The chemical weapons made your father seem as if he had lost all his senses. He acted like mad, sometimes he laughed, sometimes he cried and then he killed himself with a knife'. That was how they had seen him.

"When I reached the outdoor of the house, and tried to open it, I heard a few people outside in the alley. It sounded as though they were having a big argument, maybe fighting about something to take from the houses. When I heard this, I was scared. I tried to get back into the basement to shelter among so many dead bodies. I heard later that, when so many people were killed, their houses were plundered. I am not sure whether the argument was over looted booty or what.

"My situation was getting worse all the time until I could hardly move. I felt I was almost dead, with hardly any feeling in my limbs. I fainted. When I came round I heard a few people talking in Kurdish and heard one of them say, 'I am sorry, they are all dead.' They did not come down to the basement and I could not raise my voice to call or shout, 'I am alive!' Therefore, they left and they did not know I was there, still alive, and desperately trying to survive.

"For a third night, I was still among the dead bodies. I was very weak and barely alive. I often fainted and came round again. Once I came round and sensed there were a few people at the top of the basement, taking photos and talking in a foreign language I didn't understand. I knew they weren't Persian or Arabs because I could distinguish between those two foreign languages. I thought they were foreign reporters. I tried to see them but by then I was blind and could not use my eyes at all. I tried to call them, but I was too weak. I only managed to raise my right hand a few inches but, with my bad luck, they did not see this. It was very dark and they left me.

"The time was passing and my situation was getting worse. I could hardly manage to move my limbs and had lost my sight and was expecting death by then. I often fainted and came round. Then I heard some people speaking Persian in the basement. I only managed to move my fingers to show some sign of life, to give a signal that I was still alive. This time, someone saw me. I was picked up by two men and taken out from the basement and put into the back of a pickup car. I could hear a few more injured people in the car who were whining with pain. It seemed like the car was going around Halabja for about half an hour.

"There were many more people with injuries, and we were all sort of piled up. The car filled up with so many injured civilians. It finally stopped next to a revving machine that sounded like a helicopter.

"They were taking out the injured and putting them in the helicopter. I was conscious until they took me into the helicopter, and then I fainted. I do not know for how long I was unconscious. When I awoke, I felt two women were washing me. 'Where is this place?' I managed to ask. 'This is Kermashan'* one of the nurses replied.

 (Kermashan is a Kurdish city in Iranian part of Kurdistan)

"I stayed for nearly a month in that hospital. My health was very bad. My skin was still burning. I had lost my sight and the hair of my body. I was breathing with difficulty and coughed a lot. After a while, I felt a bit better and they sent me to another hospital, the Bahashti Hospital in Tehran. I stayed there for six months for treatment. They treated me very well. There were another four chemical attack patients in the same hospital, all young like me.

"After about six months, I felt better and was discharged and sent to the refugee camp of Sanghor, where there were mostly relatives of chemical attack victims. There were many people there from Halabja who had tried to escape the attack and the Anfal campaign.

"While I was there, the camp's officials tried to find my relatives, but I had no one there. Eventually a middle-aged man came who knew my family, and knew that my grandma was in the Hersin refugee camp. They sent me to that camp where I was reunited with my grandma - my mother's mum - and my uncle. I was with them until we went back to South Kurdistan. I stayed there until 1998 when I left my country.

"I was not sure whether Hoshman, my childhood friend, had survived. I had heard nothing from him after he kicked the bucket of dirty water and would not let me drink from it. I had seen no sign of life or movement from him after that. However, fortunately, after 24 years of separation I discovered he was alive and, on 15th August 2012, I met him after so many years of separation.

"His situation had been just like mine. All his family were lost in the Halabja chemical attack. We hugged each other with floods of tears mixed with happiness and grief.

"I still cannot understand why we were used, why we Halabja people were massacred in such a horrific way. The people of Halabja all knew Saddam was going to use chemical weapons, as he had often used them against Kurdish revolutionaries and Iranian forces". 1

1. Hashtaw Hasht, the Kurdish Magazine, Spring & Summer 2006 75 -77

2. Hashtaw Hasht, Kurdish Magazine, June & July 2006 22 -23

3. Muhamed, and eyewitness of the Chemical attack on Halabja

4.. Mr Abd Al Rahman was interviewd by the Klil Kurdish Magazine in February 2004 in

   Halabja.

  5. Kamaran Nawroz story of what happened in Halabja

3. The Anfal Genocide Campaign

In 1988, when the Iran-Iraq war ended with a cease fire, the Saddam regime's Anfal campaign – the mass killing of the civilian Kurdish population - was already underway. It was one of the most fearsome campaigns designed to wipe out Kurds from the surface of their own homeland. It was exactly like Adolf Hitler and his German Nazis did in sending millions of Jews to concentration camps to exterminate them.

Anfal is the name of a verse or 'sura' of the Quran, referring to the 'spoils of war' - the plunder taken from defeated enemies as happened in the Tabuk war.

* 'The word Anfal in Arabic means booty, a justified plunder in war, because for the ones who fought and refused to convert to Islam, their killing was justified and their properties were considered legitimate war gains taken by the tribal Arab armies.' In the holy Quran, the word Anfal is in the eighth sura and contains 75 verses. It came down to prophet Muhamed in the Ramadan of the second year of the lunar calendar during the Badre War.' 1

The first political division of Kurdistan was agreed upon in 1514, between the Safavid Persians and

Ottoman Turks. This was not fully implemented because of the continued animosity between Persians and Ottomans, and the Kurds used this division to their advantage whenever opportunities arose. The next time, Kurdistan was divided into four parts - based on the Sykes-Picot agreement - between the victors of the First World War. The repression of Kurds has continued ever since.

All the subsequent regimes in Iraq followed the same policy of depriving Kurds of their basic human rights. The Ba'athist regime that came to power in 1968 was one of the most barbarous in the Middle East since the Armenian massacre carried out by Turkey in 1915. The Ba'athists pursued their policy of repression, extermination and ethnic cleansing as soon as they took power in a coup d'etat.

As they tightened their grip on power in Baghdad, they acted not only against Kurds but also against all religious and ethnic minorities and their political opponents. One of their first steps was the campaign of Ba'athification to enforce a change of identity of Kurds, as part of their racist and nationalist policy of glorifying the Arab race. In response to this, Kurds took up arms and started fighting back against the Ba'athist regime.

Between 1961 and 1968 the Iraqi people saw five changes in the government of Iraq, all of which followed the same policy of depriving Kurds and the other minorities of their basic human rights. The policy of discrimination, repression, arrest, torture and killing of Kurds and other minority groups amounted to the crime of genocide as defined by the UN on 9th December 1948.

The term genocide was first used by the Polish writer Raphael Lemkin in 1944, and it appeared in the indictment of Nazi war criminals at Nuremburg trial in 1945. Lemkin was the principle drafter of the 1948 UN Conventions for the Prevention and Punishment of Genocide. .2.

The general assembly of the United Nations, in response to the horrors of the Second World War , declared in its resolution of 11th December 1946 that genocide "is a crime under international law, contrary to the support and designs of the United Nations, and condemned by the civilised world." Genocide received further analysis by the United Nations' Economic and Social Council, which appointed a special committee and approved the 9th December 1948 Convention against Genocide. According to Article 2 of the Convention, genocide means any of the following acts committed with intent to destroy, in whole, or in part, a national, ethnic, racial, or religious group:

- Killing members of the group

- Causing serious bodily or mental harm to members of the group

- Deliberately inflicting on the group conditions of life calculated to bring about its physical destruction completely, or in part

- Imposing measures intended to prevent births within the group

- Forcibly transferring children of the group to another place

The Ba'athists' first step in their campaign of genocide was the mass relocation of 300,000 Kurds, mainly civilians, to South Iraq after the 1975 Algeria Pact, when the Kurdish Revolution was brought to its knees with the support of the Soviet Union, USA and Arabs states backing the Ba'athist regime.

The next step was to destroy more than 4,000 villages in the areas bordering Iran and Turkey, and relocate the villagers to concentration camps guarded around the clock.

 Another stage of their campaign of ethnic cleansing, on 31st July 1983, was the process of extermination of the Barzani people, when the regime's forces raided their concentration camp at Qushtapa near Erbil. The Iraqi army took away 8,000 Barzani males above the age of seven. After the downfall of

Saddam, the bodies of 503 out of thousands of murdered Barzanis were discovered in a mass grave in the deserts of southern Iraq.

On 4th May 1985, the regime started its campaign of ethnic cleansing against the Faili Kurds who had lived in East Baghdad as Iraqi citizens for generations. The campaign against the Faili Kurds started with deportations, as they claimed the Faili Kurds were originally Iranian and so should go back to Iran. The regime occupied and plundered their properties. These deportations, exile and plunder amounted to the crime of genocide.

On 16th April 1987, the regime deployed WMD on the Ballisan valley, using chemical weapons against Kurdish guerrilla forces and hundreds of civilian villagers who were massacred.

On 19th February 1988, when the first stage of the mass Anfal campaign started, the regime used its armed forces to plunder and destroy hundreds of villages, arresting all the villagers. This campaign lasted until 7th September 1988

This Anfal campaign against the Iraqi Kurds was waged in several phases in the following areas:

 1. The town of Kfrie and surrounding villages

2. The town of Kalar and the plain of Garmyian and villages

3. The town of Derbandikhan and villages

4. The town of Khanaqin and villages

5. The town of Dubz and villages

6. The Kirkuk Kurds, and the Kurdish villages in the Kirkuk area; the town of Chemchemal town and villages

7. The Qaradagh region, Slemani villages and the Jafaiety valley villages

8. The town of Koisenjaq and villages

9. The town of Shaqlawa, Erbil, and the surrounding villages

10. The massacre of 60 families, comprising 500 civilians, following their return from Iran to Halabja, where they were victims of the chemical attack

11. Amed and Aqra town and villages

12. The Dahouk villages, during the Bahdinan Anfal Campaign

All told these Anfal campaigns involved the murder of more than 182,000 civilians. Among the victims, in many mass graves, were children who were buried alive, sometimes clutching toys in their hands, and babies born only to be buried alive.

All the Kurds' herds, Cattles, orchards and properties were plundered, and their villages burnt to the ground. These inhuman acts caused massive environmental damage. Until after the downfall of Saddam's regime, the fate of these people was unknown to their surviving loved ones. After the fall of Saddam, dozens of mass graves were discovered in the deserts of southern Iraq. When Saddam was finally caught by the allied forces and put on trial with his diabolical cousin Ali Hassan Majeed, better known as Chemical Ali, there were documents and witnesses aplenty. Among the evidence was a mass grave that was discovered holding 358 corpses of Kurdish families, including children, in the area called Hazar, near Samawa in the South of Iraq.

It was well known that Chemical Ali once grabbed hold of an infant from a Kurdish family and hurled the baby at a tank, saying, "We want to get rid of this race".

1.   Hashtawhasht, the Kurdish magazine, 2006, Slemani

2.   Charny 1988 1, du press 1994, 7

A. Taimoor, a 12 year old boy, Only Survivor of the Garmyan Anfal Campaign

Taimoor Ahmad, was a twelve year boy in 1988, when Saddam's Anfal campaign started, in South Kurdistan.

This is a summary of a translated version of his interview with the Kurdish journalist Aref Qurbani which appeared in his book, 'Taimoor, Only Survivor of the Anfal Campaign'.

"My name is Taimoor Ahmad. I was born on 1st January 1976. My mother's name is Sarah Muhamed Mahmoud, from the village of Kullajo in Kalar region. We were a family of six: my mum, dad, three sisters and I. We were a very happy life. How can I forget them? We were very close family, like most Kurds having very strong family and social relations.

"I will never forget my family until the day of judgement, when we may meet up again. My family, all of them, were very handsome. My father was from the Rokhzayie tribe, with his big moustache, and with his black and white turban. My mum was very beautiful, tanned, slim, and with sweet features. My sisters took after my dad, light skin, tall, dark eyes and dark brown hair. I was the eldest child; my sisters Gielas, Snoor and Lawlaw were born after me.

"Our village was about forty-five houses; we had no electricity and tap water. We had our spring water source, and some of us had a well. Sometimes in late spring, when the spring water source ran out, we used the wells to get water. We had a small primary school, and I was there with about 20 pupils in my class. All of my school friends: Azad, Saman, Sirwan and Ata, were caught in the Anfal campaign. They were all shot dead by the Iraqi soldiers. I think none of them survived the mass killing.

"My father was a farmer. We moved to the town of Kalar for a while, but when my father was called up to the Iraqi army – to put it in an official way – to go to war, he did not go. He refused to get involved in the senseless killing of war. "Why should I kill anyone?" he said. He refused to go, and we moved back to the village. I learned about this when he talked with relatives and neighbours. I was too young to understand what was really going on.

"I remember my childhood, when many things happened. How could I forget the mass killing of our neighbours, family, relatives, and my classmates? At the time, I did not understand why anything like this should happen to us, or to anyone.

"I remember when I was very young, when the Iraqi army often came to our village, killed our people, and a helicopter gunship was shooting us. They burnt my uncle Khursheed's car. Another time they bombed and burnt a pick-up car that belonged to Mr Ata Hadji Hamajan. Oh, I watched as it was burning, and I wondered why. I did not understand. I cannot remember the exact dates of those dreadful events. No, I cannot remember all of them, but I clearly remember when I saw the helicopters and tanks, and soldiers who were aiming their guns at us. At the time, it seemed like it was the era of death, with bombing and fighting all the time. When the revolutionaries, the peshmarga – Kurdish freedom fighters – came, they took the tractors and cars of the village; they took them to get around. As soon as the government knew that they were around, they started bombing us with long-range artillery bombs.

"Especially at night, if they happened to see any tractors or cars headlights, they would start bombing our villages. In addition, during the day, they would send their helicopter gunships, to bomb and shoot at us. Why they were doing this? These were our homes, villages, country – why were they coming? I could not make out why. I was too young. Overall, our life was miserable.

"We could not lead a normal life, especially if one was an army deserter. My dad was one: he did not go to war and so we were always worried. As I got older, I began to understand more and grew anxious. I had a fear that, if they arrested dad, they would shoot him. All the family was worried that, one day, he might be caught and killed by the Arab army.

"I remember when our people heard that the army and jash mercenaries were coming. All the army deserters and those known to be involved with peshmarga groups were running away to hide. They dug up places, tunnels underground, to go and hide. My father was one of them. I often went with him, we were very close to each other, and I always wanted to be with him. Some of his friends were annoyed when they saw me. They were worried that I might make a noise and give them away, and so all of us would be murdered by the Iraqi soldiers.

"Even when my dad went to the other villages with his daily chores, he took me with him. We were very close. I even helped him with his farming and looked after the herd of sheep. We were very happy, all my family, we all loved each other. We enjoyed every minute of being together, it was a heaven of life, if they just let us live, but they did not. I often thought, even when there was a war, if you are with loved ones, your worries are less. Even though our village life was very difficult and dangerous, I thought our family togetherness healed most of the wounds of anxiety and fear.

"Even before I was born, my father said, our village was often under attack, from artillery bombs, tanks and the Iraqi air force. I did not know why even our shepherd with the herd was shot dead by the government forces. Our farmers were just doing their farming and they had no guns but the helicopters shot them dead. I did not understand why the government was doing this. I remember that, when the men were going to town and the kids wanted to go with them, the elders would often say, 'No, you can't come, the government soldiers will arrest you'. That was how they put them off. That was how we were brought up with fear.

"As our life was always a war and we were fearful of an attack, my father had a Kalashnikov gun. Many of our villagers had one, but not all, only those who could afford one. The peshmarga forces liked this.

"I remember once there was a fight between the government forces and the peshmarga gunmen in the village of Sarqalla, near our village. I went with my dad and my uncle Osman to have a look, from a hillside near our village. We saw from far away, there was something like fireballs and we heard thunder-like noise. I asked my father, 'What happens if an artillery bomb comes to hit us?'

"'It is just the thunder bolt, don't worry.' he replied.

"He knew I was scared and, after a few minutes, he said, 'Let's go home'. That night I was scared, I could not sleep, my dad came and cuddled me in bed. I heard the sound of explosions coming closer. My father fell asleep but I did not. After a while, there was a big explosion, which made everyone wake up. When my dad opened the door, we saw a fire on the hill where we had been watching the fight earlier. My father looked at me and said, 'It was good that we listened to you and came home'. It did not take long before another bomb exploded nearby, and then we all went into the bomb-shelter under our front hall.

"Inside, the bomb-shelter was damp but my mum brought a sack of wheat & barley straws and scattered it around to make it more comfortable for us. A bit later, we found out that the big explosion had hit the house of Rustam Hamajan, killing his wife and two children and wounding another child. I felt shivers in my body when I remembered that.

"No one could fall asleep that night. In the morning, all the villagers got together to help bury the dead. After the burial ceremony, we all left the village, as we feared that the government would come back to bomb us. It had happened many times, we all knew this, that when the villagers left their houses and the government came, they plundered all the houses. When they were busy with looting and taking our properties, they left us alone for a while.

"We were unaware of what was happening in the other villages, as there was no electricity and TV in our village. We did not know when the army would come back to attack us. A few families had radios, but the available stations never mentioned what was happening, as the government did not allow any media coverage to come into the area. They not only looted our property and houses, they even set them on fire. They burnt our harvest and took our cattle and sheep herds.

"We gradually became stranded, as we were not allowed to leave, or to settle in the other towns and cities. We were not able to go anywhere and we were worried. Even the Kurdish revolutionaries did not like it if we abandoned our villages. The ones who wanted to leave, they did not let anyone know. They would try to leave secretly. However, there was a risk: if we were caught, we would not know what was going to happen to us, and we knew that we could not hide in the fields anymore.

"There was no way to defend our villages, no forces left in the area. The government was ready with its air force, tanks and thousands of soldiers. Every day was becoming worse for us, especially when we realised that the Iraqi army's tanks and soldiers had surrounded all our villages. We thought that was it, we were finished, with no way to escape.

"We hoped that we could reach one of the cities. We tried through one of the jash leaders, hoping that he would be able to help us to get to the Smoud camp. This was near the town of Kalar and it was where some villagers had been gathered by the regime. Those of us who decided to take that route boarded three tractors, with some essential household belongings, and we headed to Tilaco village to get nearer to the Smoud camp.

"Tilaco, a bigger village, it was about fifteen minutes from ours. The rest of our villagers stayed at home. After we set off, we heard the army bombing our village. They shot fire flares in the sky above us. We turned our tractors headlights off and tried to hide, in case they would bomb us. We sent a few men to try to find 'Mustashar' the mercenary leader, but he could not be found. He did not show up: either he was too scared or he had lied to us.

"The night in Tilaco was very scary. We were very tired and hardly slept. The next day we needed to head towards Mlasura village. It was only a 30-family village, and we had to take all our food with us, as they already had many guests from other villages. It took us about half an hour to arrive, and the army did not come yet. Oh, it was such a frightening situation, it is impossible to describe, it was like the end of the world. We did not know if the way we were going would be safe enough to survive. We did not know if we should surrender ourselves or let the army arrest us. We were very desperate and had no clue what to do.

"Some of our people thought and suggested, 'If we go ourselves to the army, that would be better than if the army arrests us'. We weren't sure what to do. We stayed there for three days, and every day more people from the other villages were arriving. We really did not know why so many people were heading towards Mlasura. Whether they thought they would be saved by going there or not, I do not know.

"After the third day, the army came to Mlasura. We thought they were coming to take us to a camp to settle us somewhere else. We would be included in the government amnesty. Many people believed that this was the case. We really wanted a way out, so that the helicopter gunships would not come to shoot or bomb us anymore. We hoped that the government had built concentration camps near the towns and cities for us to settle, so that we would not be living in danger anymore.

"It had happened before, to so many other villagers, when they were relocated in collective camps, and so they would not be living under any threats of bombing, killing and plunder. Our people were very happy to leave their villages, as if they were heading towards a haven and peace because we were fed up with the life we had. The villagers' tractors were going fast, as if they were racing to reach the collective camp. We all were happy. We did not know that we all were going to be murdered.

"The transport links between the villages were very poor and that was why most of the villagers used tractors. There were hundreds that had come to the Mlasura village. I remember we felt like we were in the convoy of a wedding party, when people were enjoying the trip so much. If we had known what the government was going to do to us, we would have tried to escape from Mlasura…

"Some villagers, who had no tractors or cars and had come on foot, were put in army lorries. We found ourselves surrounded by many tanks, soldiers and helicopters. We were heading towards Quoratwo camp, which was another big village, where there was a concentration camp.

"We all thought that we would be given new houses or places to live but, on the way, we were guarded heavily. Many women came along the roadside and they all were crying, and the soldiers fired fire bullets above the crowds of families and children. When we arrived in the Smoud camp, there was no one to register anyone, or allocate them a place to stay.

"We thought it was a government amnesty. Even if we had been guilty of anything, we never expected what they were going to do to us. All these families on their journey did not know what they were going to face. Even if they considered that somehow our men were guilty of anything, why should they punish all the families, the old and the children? We were worried. Oh God, what was happening?

"When we did not stop at the Smoud camp, we were getting worried. What they were going to do with us? 'The army deserters will be taken out', we thought. They would be sent to do army service, as they needed recruits. Alternatively, if they were going to shoot them, why should the government also arrest all of the women and children? I was worried about my dad. I was worried we were going to be separated. I was thinking that, if they arrested him, I would go with him and they might show some sympathy because of me. I never wanted to be separated from him. I was also worried that, if they never released us, then my mother and sisters would be left alone, and who should look after them? Oh God, what a frightening situation it was. I was thinking, and pleading with God to save us, to release us so that we could go back to Kalar town or to the Smoud camp. 'Why does God not come to our rescue? What have we done to be punished like this?' I thought.

"When we were in the Mlasura village, we expected that the army and the jash would come to kill us all, but later when they came and did not kill us, this gave us some hope. The head of mercenaries told us, 'You will go to a camp. They will give you a place to stay'. So we felt happy, as we were reassured that they would not kill us. I was thinking that, if we settled somewhere, I would go back to school. I was in year two, but my age group were all in year five. I did not care so long as we were safe and treated well. I thought the school would consider my age and put me in a higher class. I knew I would cope, I loved going to school and learning. That was the only way to get out of this misery. 'If I was going with my sisters, I would be holding their hands to go to school,' I thought.

"We would be away from the helicopters, government tanks and soldiers, who often came to bomb us. So many times they came to burn our houses and destroy our farms. We would be somewhere where we would not be scared anymore. Nevertheless, when we were on the road, going somewhere we did not know what would happen. There were many families on the roadside and they all were crying for us. When we passed the Smoud camp, and the town of Kalar, many women came on the road and they were all crying for us. Oh God, what was happening? They must know that something bad was going to happen to us. We never knew what was going to happen.

"They took us to Quoratwo castle. It was a big castle, I had never seen anything like it. The building was made of mud bricks. It was a big place, with a big entrance. All the tractors headed in, and everyone gathered there. We all stayed there and they kept bringing more villagers.

"They did not give us any food, and only brought water in tankers. Most of the people had their own food and some household stuff. They helped out those who did not have any food. Many of the villagers had brought their sheep herds until they reached the edge of the town, and then the Iraqi army seized them all. They brought us a few tankers of water, but it was not enough, as they kept bringing more people.

"Many soldiers guarded the place; they wore greenish-grey army uniforms. Most of them had Kalashnikovs. A few had pistols and they came with lists looking for some names, or this was how it seemed. We were being held in a huge, two storey circular building and, once they brought anyone in, and there was no way to escape. No one was allowed to leave. We only learned about what was happening outside from the newcomers who came from other villages. My father listened as they brought news of where the army was and how many villages had been destroyed and looted.

"I do not know if anyone tried to escape but, as I went with my father to the top of the castle, we saw that thousands were on their way towards the Quoratwo castle. It looked as though all of the Garmyan area villages had been destroyed, and all the villagers arrested. I once heard my father tell my uncle, 'If it was not for my family, I would have escaped'. I was very sad for my father, because he wanted to escape, but he would never want to leave us behind.

"I wish we had gone to my uncle, when he sent a message telling my father to surrender and go to the army. He was not sure: it was a big war and he thought he would be killed somewhere for the Arabs. My father was also worried about us. If he had left, what would have happen to us? However, I wish he had gone, anyway. As I later discovered that, no matter what we did, as far as the government was concerned, we were Kurds, and we all had to die.

"For about ten days, we all were kept in the Quorato camp. On the eleventh day, they brought big lorries and started loading them up with the detained villagers. They had a list of names and they wanted to group together people from the same family or the same village. They were transferring us to the Topzawa village army barrack near Kirkuk. I think it took them about 10 days to transfer all the Garmyan villagers. The villagers had to leave all their tractors behind, in the Quoratwo village with the Iraqi army, and every lorry had a guard with a gun.

"All the villager children were scared of the Iraqi soldiers. They were like angels of death, and wherever we met them, they almost killed us. As they came near us, we all were scared, crouched down and trembled with fear.

"When we left Quorato, we did not know where we would end up. We had left most of our belongings and just taken our food and some clothes. On the way, one of my cousins was very thirsty and she picked up a container of kerosene, thinking it was water, and drank from it. She started coughing and vomiting. My father desperately banged on the rooftop of the lorry, to try and make it stop. When we were near an army barracks, we stopped and my father took her to the army clinic to get some treatment.

"The whole convoy stopped and, when many villagers got off, the soldiers panicked and forced them back onto the lorries. We were delayed for about three hours. When we reached Topzawa village, it was like a hell. It was a big army camp, fenced with barbed wire. They separated us in groups according to our age and sex. All the younger ones were separated, and the old were put on one side. We were put in different groups, and in different halls. They kept bringing more villagers on passenger buses. So many of us were gathered, God knows how many, perhaps tens of thousands.

"When they registered our names, they put my father and uncle in the men's group, separated from us. I was with my mum and my sisters in another group, and my grandma was separated from us in the group of old people.

"When they separated my dad, I held his hand tight, and tried hard to grab his hand, as I did not want to be separated from him. My father took out from his pocket fifteen dinars Iraqi currency and gave me this money. He knew they would not let me stay with him. However, I tried hard and held his hand tight. I saw tears in his eyes, but he tried not to show any emotion, and told me 'Keep that money, you may need it with your mum and sisters'.

"My father looked like he knew what was happening. We would not see each other anymore. He did not think that the government would kill all the women and children, as no one thought so. I tried hard not to let him go, I wanted to be with him, wherever he was going, but a soldier came, grabbed my arm, pushed me away and separated me from my father. We looked at each other with tears in our eyes. I just wondered why they were doing this to us. At the time I could not understand, and did not think they were going to kill all these people. They treated us worse than cattle. They kicked us and hit us with gun butts.

"In Topzawa, we lost all hope. It became obvious they would not let us go free again, when we saw that they were hitting and pushing us in a hurry to separate us from each other and towards the halls. We all knew they were going to kill all the men, but no one thought that they were also going to kill all the families and children.

"My father, when he gave me the money, never thought that would happen. He did not know that we would never be free to spend that money. He did not know they would shoot all of us. Oh God, why should anything so bad ever happen? We all thought they were Muslim and would have some faith. We thought only God would be able to save us, but he did not…

"I never forget when the soldiers forcibly separated me from my father. I saw in his facial expression, an agony of sorrow, a pain of separation, as if his facial expressions were screaming in silence. They took him where the young men were. My sisters were very young and they were scared to death, and holding on to mum's dress, as if they were hiding away from the grip of hungry wolves. I looked at mum's face and it was full of tears. My sisters too were frightened, but too scared to cry. They were holding on to mum's legs as if worried that she might run away.

"I always remember those dreadful scenes and I live with them. The soldiers took my dad away with all the males who were above fifteen years old.

"We had uncle Umar, Osman, and a few more families from Kulajo village with us until we were separated in the Topzawa army camp. As I found out later, they sent the group of old people to South Iraq, somewhere called Negrosalman. Some died there, and some returned to Kurdistan after many years.

"They were separating all the groups with kicks, pushing and hitting us, so we wouldn't think about any resistance. They searched us for anything that we had on us - even nail clippers, beads, any money, watches or anything of value. If anyone had any valuables or nice clothes they were told to take them off.

"There was hardly any food or water, not enough to go around, as there were so many of us. Sometimes, when we got the leftovers from the army barracks, cold and tasteless, we could hardly eat anything. There weren't enough toilet facilities. It was so crowded and if anyone had a chance to go, soldiers would harass them to finish quickly.

"Many could not wait, especially children, they discharged where they were standing, and everywhere was stinking. The soldiers were criminals who respected no one. I often saw soldiers kicking and pushing old men. One old man was pulled by his white beard. When a soldier kicked another old man, he fell on his face. There was blood and dust on his face but no one dared to go to help him. We all were too frightened.

"Once, when I tried to go to toilet and was in the queue, I came across a man from our village, I was so pleased to see him, and went to him and said, 'Salaam Kaka Muhamed, have you seen my dad?'

'No, I have never seen him, sorry.' He replied. His face was sad, and his reply was cold. 'Oh God, what is happening', I thought. I went back to my mum and my sisters and told them, 'I saw Muhamed and asked him about my dad'. I told them what he said, and then we all started crying…Oh God, it was so painful.

"I once saw that a woman was giving birth. A few women went to help her. They tried to cover her, not let any soldiers see her. But the soldiers came, raised the cover and looked at her, and they were laughing at her. It was so awful to see those soldiers acting like vicious animals. It was so insulting the way they behaved. What an unfortunate day to give birth to an infant, to be born into the hands of criminals with intent to kill.

"Those days in Topzawa we witnessed many horrible scenes. I wondered why they were so cruel. I remember that, when the peshmaga forces brought a few captured soldiers to our village, they never harmed them at all, and they were given food and shelter and treated with respect. I could not understand why we were being treated like this. We were not peshmarga gunmen (or, as they called them, mukharibine or terrorists). Why they do all these horrible things to us? I remember in our Kurdish villages, whenever we had strangers, travellers or even the Iraqi army around, we invited them into our homes, cooked for them and looked after them. We never had cafes, restaurants or hotels, and anyone visiting our villages was always our dear guest, as is the well-known tradition in the Kurdish countryside.

"With a few of my friends I went to do some cleaning for the camp halls. We cleaned in the kitchen and the toilets in order to make them have a little bit of sympathy for us. I hoped to get some food from them since I always worked hard to please them. Once, a soldier called me to give me some food with meat/ I was delighted to get this and hoped to take it to my mum and sisters.

"However, when I got close to the plate, the soldier kicked it away from my hand and did not let me eat from it or take it away. 'Oh God what a criminal he is. They have no fear of God.' I thought. I did not understand why they were so hateful. We would never do that, even to animals.

"One day, when I was doing some cleaning, I came across a hall full of the villager's belongings: clothes, watches, beads, lighters, and many other personal items. These items belonged to our people, and they were being stripped of any valuables and belongings before they took them to the execution desert.

"They took all the villagers away in big white buses. They were strange white buses with seats back to back. We could not see the driver, as his place was separate from us. They took us to the execution area in the desert in South Iraq. All the buses were crammed with our people.

"They did not care whether we were comfortable or not. In our bus were our family, my auntie Mahssum and her ten children, and Hamdyia my other auntie. There were my uncle, Osman's family and many women from our village, including Piroz Hasan Mirweis's wife and her children. Her husband used to be my granddad's shepherd. I do not know what happened to him. I remember there was a heavily pregnant woman with us. On the way she fell ill and collapsed. Froth was coming out from her mouth. I gave her some water, and she uttered a few words. She thanked me, and pleaded for God's protection.

"We had all my cousins with us: Sardar, Kamal, Jamal, and Shamal. They were all my age group friends, and we were at the same school. There were many more girls and boys from my village, we all were friends. On the way in the bus, there were too many of us, with hardly any air, and no proper window to see where they were taking us. It was very hot. We had a little window, and a very small gap to get some air. As we were so tired and hungry and did not have enough water, two of the children died on the way.

"The driver never stopped to see what was happening. We put the two corpses aside, and then we were waiting for our death. It now seemed inevitable we all were going to die. The children who were dead were about eight or nine years old. We had been travelling from the evening before, and had no food or water, apart from a container of drinking water that my auntie had with her. We all were pleading with God to come to our rescue. There was no fresh air, it was getting hotter and we were dehydrated, thirsty, hungry and getting dizzy. We were desperate to stop somewhere. Even if they would kill us, we just wanted some fresh air. We felt as though we were being suffocated, and we did not know why we were being punished like this. We had no sins, most of us were just children; we had no idea about the politics of the day, and what was going on.

"We were travelling for hours, and felt as if we would never arrive. From Topzawa to the deserts of Samawa in South Iraqi desert was about 600 miles. That was why it took us so long to arrive. We were locked in the bus, and we could not open the doors at all; otherwise, a few of us would have jumped off. After many hours of travelling, it felt as if the bus had left the paved road and we were going somewhere bumpy and unpaved. We were on the country roads, and the bus was not going steady anymore. When the bus suddenly came to a halt, we got off and were told to wait. They saw the two children who were dead and told us to leave them there.

"At first, I was pleased to get fresh air. But then I looked around at the grey sky, and the limitless expanse of desert, and noticed that the soil under our feet was different. It was just soft sand, not like our home soil. I was very scared, 'Are they going to leave us all here?' I thought and I looked around. Everyone was just like me, staring at the gloomy empty desert. They were just like me, worried about what was going to happen. 'They will leave us all here in the desert without food and water, to die in the dry desert heat', I thought.

"I did not know that we did not deserve even to be left in the desert. They had brought us all there to be shot dead. Many more buses were arriving and it was nearly evening sunset. There was no army barracks. There were just a few Toyota cars that had accompanied us. They brought a water container, and gave some water to each of us. 'That is the only kindness we have seen from them,' we naively thought. It was strange. We still did not know why they brought us to that empty desert, and what they were going to do to us.

"For that little sip of water, our women were very grateful to them. I do not know why we were so naive as to be deceived with a little bit kindness. It did not take long before they brought plain pieces of black cloth to tie around our eyes, to blindfold us.

"After a while, they made us get in the bus again and drove us further into the desert. Everyone else on the bus was blindfolded, but I was not. I did not know why. I could have opened my mum's and my sisters' blindfold black knots, but I did not. I was very scared. They drove us further into the desert for about ten minutes, and then stopped again. They let us off, this time it looked like this was it. This was to be our last moments of life.

"When I got off, I saw that the buses were each parked beside a dug-out hole in the desert. All the villagers were standing next to the holes, and we all were panicking. Oh God, this is it. No one uttered a word. When I later remembered, I thought, 'The little water they gave us was some chemicals, perhaps poisonous water to make us dizzy and lose our sense of awareness and fear, because we were dizzy, and not fully conscious of what was going on'.

"I had never before seen mechanical shovels used to make holes in the ground, but the desert ground was so soft and that was why they used them. They had dug out many holes, each was about 6 metres by 5 metres: 30 square metres.

"I remember that, when they ordered us to get into the hole, my auntie fell in and died. Perhaps she had a heart attack. I did not know but she was already dead before any shooting started. Still no one uttered a word. It was better to have a heart attack than being shot like that. We had done nothing wrong to deserve being shot like that. It was strange to put all of us into one grave. There was no burial ceremony and each group was in a huge grave. We felt as though we were all suffocated; short of breath, we could hardly breathe. I was next to my mum holding onto her dress. We crouched as though trying to make ourselves smaller, and trembled with fear. It was sunset, but not dark yet.

"A soldier brought the bodies of the two children who had died in the bus on the journey, and threw them into our hole, before they shot us. Next to each dug-out hole was a soldier with a Kalashnikov gun. They had special commando uniforms of green with dark or brown patterns, and they had black boots on. They were holding their guns with one hand and, with the other hand, their index fingers were on the triggers, aimed their guns at us.

"As we all were innocent, and had done nothing wrong, I thought God would not let them kill us just like that. We were waiting for God's mercy and sympathy. The soldiers were standing on heaps of sand. They seemed high above us, and they aimed their guns at us.

"For about ten minutes after we were ordered into the dug-out holes we were waiting to be killed. I heard someone order them to start shooting us. That was why they all started together. It sounded as if they were emptying all their magazines, of 30 bullets each, and twice changed their magazines and pressed the triggers.

"They sprayed all of us with volleys of bullets. It was strange, as if I was supposed to see all that happening. I often remember those scenes: there is no way to escape from thinking about them. They never leave my sight, my mind. I was staring at what was happening, panic-stricken. I was looking at the soldiers who sprayed all the families and children with bullets. They started quickly. There was no slow shooting to aim at one person at a time. They sprayed us with many volleys of gunshots.

"As we were being shot, everyone was falling over each other in the space of a few seconds. I saw how the soldier had shot most of the people in our group, and how they fell. I saw when my mum was shot dead. She had a white scarf, and the bullet blew her white scarf away. She fell, and blood was squirting from her head. I saw blood was coming down her cheek. Many bullets were coming quickly, I saw my sister Lawlaw, a bullet hit her face and she fell. My other sister Snoor, it was as if she was trying to fend off bullets with the palm of her hand to protect herself. A bullet hit her hand, blood darted out of it, and she fell on my mum's body. However, my other sister Geilas, I did not see how she was shot. She fell on the other side of my mum. I saw her body lying next to mum. I saw another bullet hit my other sister's arm and she fell and curled her body too.

"Another woman, who was my mum's friend, fell forward. She was crouching, as if she was in the position to say a prayer. I saw bullets hit her hip and pieces of flesh and blood fly around. I heard my uncle's wife, Amina Ali Aziz, calling my mum's name, fall to her death also. When the shooting started, all the people were falling like autumn leaves, falling over each other's bodies. Perhaps there were children who were covered by the weight of many bodies. Even if they were not caught by any bullets, perhaps they were suffocated to death.

"The Kalashnikov shooting stopped. I only heard the sound of blood, and then I do not know what made me get up and go to the soldier who was shooting us. I attacked that soldier who had killed my mum and my sisters. I did not know what I was going to do to him, I just went for him. Was I pleading with him or was I angry? I caught his waist belt very tight. I looked up to his face. I saw the soldier's eyes filled with tears. I remembered the time when my father left me and I tried to hold his hand so tight. The soldier lost the grip of his gun, as the gun was slack in his hand and was pointing downward. He had two magazines of bullets tied together with a black tape. I heard one of his superiors shout at him in Arabic. I guessed he told him off and ordered him to shoot me. Then the soldier grabbed my arm and threw me back into the pile of bodies of my family, relatives and friends. They all were my loved ones....

"It was strange that the soldier almost burst into tears when I was grabbing his belt, but he still threw me back onto the pile of corpses. I heard again someone else shouting at him as if to make him shoot me. He did shoot me, and I got a bullet or more. I do not know, my back was wounded and I fell and fainted, or at least I died for a while. When I awoke, there was no one around, only a mechanical digger, a bit further away. It seemed that it was busy trying to cover the bodies of the villagers in the many dug-out holes. I was worried in case there was anyone around who might have seen that I was still alive.

"I tried to get up. Around me there were pools of blood. It was slippery, the blood was soaked into the sand. All my family, my mum, sisters, aunties, relatives, villagers and school friends were murdered. I tried quickly to get out. I was bleeding myself and with severe pain. I was scared and it was getting dark. I looked around. The mechanical digger was still far away. I got out of our hole, still looking around at where I was. I was worried in case any soldiers were there and they would shoot me.

"I did not know where I was heading. There were shrubs, thorny shrubs, sand and nothing else. The shrubs looked like dark heaps. I was scared in case they were soldiers with guns ready to shoot me. Imagine, a 12-year old boy, wounded and bleeding, surrounded by all these threats and with severe pain, but still trying to survive.

"I saw a car's headlights and tried to hide, thinking, 'That must be the soldiers who shot us, who sprayed my whole world of love and happiness, all my people, with bullets'. There were places with piles of car tyres, lying deep in the sand and I hid myself in one of them. I saw the white land cruiser car coming around, there was one man in it, in army uniform, and he did not see me. He was looking around, perhaps looking to kill anyone who might still be alive.

"When the car had passed by, I got up and fell down. I did not know if I fainted or fell asleep. I did not know for how long. I was not aware of myself. I heard someone near me, a man in a white dress. He was calling me, 'Taimoor. Taimoor, wake up, let us go,' he sounded like my dad. Oh I was happy to hear him calling me. I got up and looked around, but no one was there, the man had disappeared. I was not sure what was happening. Was it just my imagination? Was I hallucinating?

"I tried to walk and was passing another hole with many corpses when I saw someone moving. I looked, and saw it was the movement of a child. I called, 'Who is that?' In the headlight of the mechanical digger, I saw a little child, a girl about seven or eight years old. I whispered to her, 'What are you doing? Come with me, let's go'. I urged her to come with me. 'No, no I do not want to leave my mum; I am scared of soldiers. No, I cannot leave my mum. My legs are stuck under her. No, I am not coming', she said. I left her. I did not know what to do. I was too young to understand that I should not have left her alone.

"I was so scared. I could not do anything about the girl, and was scared that if we talked, there might be soldiers around to hear us and we would give ourselves away. I tried to go somewhere, every dark heap of sand or shrubs became like a soldier, as if they were pointing their guns at me. I tried to think what to do. I thought that I should follow the tracks of car tyres in the sand. I tried to feel the sand and take a route. I remembered that we were not too far from the paved road when earlier we had come by bus. I kept trying to follow a route, but often lost it and tried to find another one.

"I was tired, bleeding, thirsty and hungry. I still pleaded with God to save me, I was scared if I saw any car headlights that they were probably soldiers who would shoot me. I kept on going until I saw a fire in the dark, in the distance. I headed towards it. 'I will try and see if they are not soldiers', I thought. I plodded along, and got nearer. Suddenly I saw moving heaps of dark shadows, and there were dogs around me. They surrounded me, big dogs. I was scared that they were going to attack and kill me, because I had a wound bleeding from my waist and perhaps that would make them tear me to pieces. I was scared. They all were barking at me. I tried to find stones to hit them with, to protect myself. I hurled a stone at one of them, to make them keep away from me and it made a screeching noise.

"I saw someone coming with a torch. It was a man, an Arab man. He dismissed the dogs and took my hand. I was somewhat pleased, as he kept the dogs away from me and took me with him. He took me to a tent. In the tent, there was an old woman and a young girl. They took me in, changed my clothes, and washed my wound which was painful. They tried to clean my stains and put some oil on my wounds. They brought me a loose 'dizdasha' , an Arab dress. They took away my bloody clothes; they brought me some yoghurt drink and bread, as I was very hungry.

"I was so tired by then, and hungry. I ate and fell asleep where I was lying…

"The next day, they brought a pickup car and took me away to somewhere else. The old woman and I were at the back of the car. She covered me with her dark overall. She tried to hide me from soldiers. When we came across police and army checkpoints, they stopped us. 'Why were you driving so fast?' a soldier asked. 'Our lady is ill, we are trying to get her to hospital', the driver replied. They did not let the soldiers see me. The car was high up and, when they had a look, they could not see me. We were on the

way for a long time, a few hours' drive. We reached
a town. I imagined it was like Kalar, my town, and I
was happy I was going home. However, suddenly I
remembered: what home? 'My mum and sisters
were all murdered and probably my dad too, as he
has disappeared and I will never saw him again.' I
thought.

"I did not know his language, but the man who
saved me from the dogs knew a bit of Kurdish, as he
had done army service in the Mosul area, and so he
understood me quite a bit and helped a lot to ease
my pains. I could not tell them anything about what
had happened until a few months later, when they
had taught me Arabic. The town I had taken for
Kalar was Samawa, in South Iraq.

"In Samawa, they left me with a family. It was a big
family, with children my age, and I had friends then.
On the way to Samawa, we stopped somewhere.
The man in the car went to a shop and bought me a
watch and gave it to me. I took mine off - it was
broken - and I wore the new one. I was pleased.
With such gestures, I understood that they cared for
me. There was no threat to my life anymore.

"One day, a young man came home and, when I saw
him in army uniform, like those who had shot us,
and sprayed us with bullets, I was scared and ran
away to hide under a table. This made the whole

family cry. They understood why I was so scared of soldiers. All the family gathered around me and started crying. The soldier changed his uniform, and he came to me and gave me some cake and soft drink, as if to show that his presence was not a threat to my life".

It took Taimoor a few months to learn Arabic, and then he told his story to the Arab family. At first, they did not let him go out, in case anyone found out who he was, because the family had a few Ba'athist neighbours. When they had any visitors, they kept Taimoor in a different room by himself. Later on, whenever he went out, he was told not talk to anyone apart from the family who had risked their lives to shelter him.

That family would have been punished if the government had found out that they were sheltering a child from the Anfal campaign. It was two years before Taimoor made contact with his uncles in Kalar. The Arab family looked after him and cared for him like one of their own.

.

 Summary of Taimoor's book, 'Taimoor, the only Survivor of the Garmyan Anfal Campaign.' published in the Kurdistan Region, Iraq, Karo Publishing, Slemani, and KRG 2013.

See also the Al-Jazeera documentary 'Kulajo: My Heart is Darkened' by Gwynne Roberts

B. The Barzani Genocide Campaign, 1975-1988

Many of the Kurds deported following the 1975 Algiers Pact faced a campaign of genocide, especially the Barzani villagers. Thousands of them were forced to leave their mountain villages and their green, agricultural lands and their herds of sheep and cattle - which were plundered by the Arab Iraqi army - and relocate to the 'Affach' area near the city of Diwanyia in South Iraq.

The Barzani villagers forced to evacuate their 76 villages were from the tribes of Barozie, Harkei and Nzari and the rest were from the Mazouri and Shirwani villages. This campaign of relocation and evacuation is considered one of the most terrible aspects of the regime's genocide campaign and, from 1975 until the end of 1976, more than 300,000 Kurds were forcibly sent to deserts of South Iraq.

After a few years, most deportees were allowed to go back to Kurdistan / North Iraq - apart from the Barzani people. The new environment of desert, dirty water, heat, hunger and disease caused the death of many, especially children and the old. Any of the local Arabs who showed any sympathy or tried assist the Barzani Kurds were severely punished and dismissed from their jobs.

One of the most atrocious afflictions imposed on the Barzani people was unemployment and poverty. Life was harsh, as they were not used to hunger, salty water and the heat of the desert. It was so hard for the Barzani people who were used to a prosperous life of farming and cattle breeding. The few who were allowed to find jobs, could only get low-paid menial work. No one could get any job without the permission of the Iraqi regime's security service.

A group of the Barzanis were separated from the rest and they disappeared. Some years later they were found to have been used in experiments involving Saddam's 'weapons of mass destruction' (WMD) such as nerve gas, Sarin, cyanide, and germ agents.

From among the few Barzanis who survived the Anfal campaign, a woman named Khedija Mustafa said:

"We were in our villages, leading a normal way of life, and one day in the morning we saw our village was surrounded by many soldiers. They did not let anyone out, and after a while they brought army Eva-lorries and carried all the villagers away to Erbil. On the way, we were hungry and thirsty. They did not give us any food or water; they cared not what we needed. In Erbil, we ended up in an army barracks.

"The next day, we were on the way again. They never told us where we were going. We travelled for about twenty-four hours, and eventually ended up somewhere. It was a flat land, a desert, with a few tents. We were scared, and thought they were going to bury us all alive or dump us in a dirty river. There were a few tents, or straw shacks. There was a dirty river, which stunk with the dead bodies of dogs and cats. The environment in the area was so bad, and our children were falling ill with diarrhoea and stomach pains. There were hardly any doctors or clinics. I lost my little son and my mother in-law. They were buried somewhere. I never saw their graves; I was not allowed to visit their graves. In the barren desert, many villagers were dying every week. At the side of our camp a signpost said, 'The House of Disappearance.'"

 Another woman who survived, Samyia Shamzin Saidew, has told her story.

"On 25th November 1975, at about 10 am, there were three helicopter gunships above the mountains near our village. One headed to the village of Argush and the other two headed to the village of Drie. When they landed, the soldiers came and surrounded our village. They did not let anyone out, apart from a few children who they sent to get some men to come back to the village.

 "The Iraqi forces stayed overnight. They separated the men and tied their arms and took them into the village school. It was snowing; there was half a meter of snow on the ground. The village was situated close to Turkey's border in the East. A few men escaped and crossed the Turkish border. The day after, all the families were rounded up and they did not let anyone take any food with them. They forced us to leave all our herds and they did not let us feed or water the herd.

"The army took us in helicopters to Miergasoor, a little town in the Erbil region. In the afternoon, they put us into Eva army lorries headed towards the plain of Erbil. The morning after, we were in Erbil. We did not know we were in Erbil and, without any food or water, we passed the day. In the evening, they put us in lorries and onto the road for two more days. They never told us where we were going. At last, we ended up in a desert which they called Jahish desert. It was near the Affach, Diwanyia, in South Iraq. We arrived at about 9 am, and we saw many other Barzani villagers who the army had brought there a few weeks before.

"We were happy to see our people; they kindly started collecting bread and food for us. When we stayed in the barren desert, we came to understand that this was the beginning of a disaster. It was so hard to get used to living in the barren desert. It was so hard to leave our beautiful green mountainous region of Kurdistan, with clear sweet water, and cool air and plenty of homemade products, for an area that was flat, dry, salty and horrible. The sky was grey, the horizon was dusty, and the desert wind blew sand-dust in our faces.

"It did not take long to feel the impact; many of us were falling ill with diarrhoea and stomach pain. Because the water was dirty, and without any medical treatment, about ten of us were dying daily, especially women, children and the old. We had no source of earning, no jobs, except the job of burying our dead. I buried my son Rasheed and my daughter Lazgeen and many other relatives. This was the place where this group of Barzani people lived and died between 1975 and 1980".

The Genocide of Barzani People 1975 -1980 p.250 – 252, Barzanyian in 20th Century by Rebuar Ramazan Abdulla, first edition, KRG 2011

In 1987 the people of 74 villages were deported from the area of Shirwana in the Mergasoor region. In this area there were the tribes of Mzoori,

Shirwani and Gardi. The occupants of another 26 villages in the area around the little town of Pirani were sent to the concentration camps of Hareer, Dyiana and Quorato. When these unfortunates were deported, their villages were razed to the ground, and their water sources and water springs were blown up with TNT bombs and cemented over with concrete.

In 1975, many Barzani villages were destroyed and razed to the ground. Villagers were taken to the concentration camp of Qushtapa, which was guarded round the clock. Furthermore, the regime's air force bombed this camp several times, and they tried to blame the Islamic Republic of Iran because, during the Iraq-Iran war, their air forces often bombed each other's towns and cities. 17 women, children and old people were killed and 50 wounded when the Iraqi regime bombed this camp on 24th September 1980. They blamed the Iranians and they also attacked some refugee camps in Iran that were sheltering Barzani people.

On 30th July 1983, the Iraqi forces surrounded the Qushtapa camp and rounded up all the male villagers over the age of seven, leaving the women and children. When a child tried hard to go with his father, the Iraqi soldiers shot the child. The boy was badly wounded and a few months later he died from his injuries and the sorrow of losing his father.

On 10th August 1983, Iraqi forces surrounded the villagers in the Quds camp, and took away all the men and, on 1st October, 1983 , the Iraqi forces rounded up all male villagers in the Pshknei & Koi villages. In total around 8,000 Barzani males aged seven and over were taken away, among them 315 children. This data has been recorded by Amnesty International. Many of these people were buried alive in the Bosayia desert of South Iraq. The total area of this desert is 24,522 square metres and it is 5.7% of the total area of Iraq, near Samawa Municipality in South Iraq. The desert is situated in the triangular area between Iraq, Kuwait and Saudi Arabia. Following the downfall of Saddam, on 17th and 18th October 2005 hundreds of bodies were discovered in mass graves. Amongst them were the remains of many Christian villagers who had lived in the Barzan area for generations.

The Barzani and the Bahdinan people who managed to escape to neighbouring countries were stripped off their Iraqi citizenship. Many of their remaining relatives were forcibly detained or taken to the borders with Iran and Turkey, left with nothing and forced to leave the country. Thousands of villages were blown up, razed to the ground, and mined with millions of land- mines to prevent anyone from returning to live there. The villagers taken to the border were left on the edge of mined areas, without letting them know exactly where the mines were. The areas of destroyed villages were kept under watch and bombed, sometimes with chemical weapons, whenever the Iraqi forces suspected any movement.

On 25th August 1988 began the eighth stage of the Anfal genocide: the Anfal of Badinan. Many of the villagers tried to escape by crossing the border. Those who reached Turkey were treated very harshly by the Turkish 'janderma' who rounded them up, put them in lorries, and sent then to a few refugee camps where they were guarded around the clock and given dirty water, causing many to fall ill. As a result more villagers tried to get to Iran, which was already sheltering fellow Kurd refugees from Iraq. Some tried to stay in areas that had been liberated by peshmarga forces, but they were vulnerable to frequent attacks by the Iraqi army and air force. Several times the Iraqi army tried to poison their drinking water. Their shepherds were often rounded up and disappeared with their cattle. 1

1.The Genocide of Barzani People 1975 -1980 p.9 & 10, Barzanyian in 20th Century by Rebuar Ramazan Abdulla, first edition, KRG 2011 RC

 2. The Genocide of Barzani People 1975 -1980 p.250 & 252, Barzanyian in 20th Century by Rebuar Ramazan Abdulla, first edition, KRG 2011 RC

C. The Bahdinan Anfal Campaign

Kamal Umar Raheed, a Kurdish Iraqi soldier from the Battalion Commandos 72 infantry has told his story of the Bahdinan Anfal campaign, in the Dahouk region, between 25th August 1988 and 6th September 1988.

"We were in our army barrack in Mosul, when we continually heard everyday communications with senior commanders discussing our forces. The Iraqi forces in the many different parts of Iraqi Kurdistan often talked about the terrorists. 'We are going to destroy them with our special forces, the commandos', we were told.

"Our senior officers often told us in seminars: 'You should never hesitate to kill anyone from the terrorists. You have to kill all the women, children, old and young. Whoever speaks the Kurdish language should be killed. If you do not kill them, they will kill you. They are the Kurds hired by Iranians and you should never have any sympathy towards them'.

"'They are not Muslims, they never practice the religion of Islam. They never abide by our holy text, the Quran. Kurd means outlaw and bandit. Those villages we are going to attack are where the terrorists were sheltered, fed and given assistance. Those families, children, girls, boys, old and young are all assisting terrorists. You must arrest and kill all of them'".

When Kamal was interviewed by the Kurdish Magazine 'Eighty Eight' in 2006, he said, "We were five Kurds in the 72 Infantry Battalion. We often met at the weekend, or sometimes at two weekly intervals and told each other our stories about what had happened.

"It was 6th August 1988, a quiet evening, and our 72 Infantry Battalion moved towards Bamarny airport following the decision of Ali Hassan al Majid, 'Chemical Ali', to head towards the Bahdinan area.

"On the day most the army personnel were happy, as they knew they would be getting so much 'booty'. They were told to plunder, loot, arrest and kill all the villagers with no exceptions".

On the day, commandos of the 6th division of the Iraqi army occupied the Matin Mountains. The 5003 army division headed towards the Mangesh area. Kamal was based at the head office of the army barracks. He knew some names of the leaders who led these armies to execute the Bahdinan Anfal Campaign: the Battalion 72 infantry was led by Brigadier Muel; Division 1 (Fawj 1) was led by the army officer with three stars, Amer Muhamed Salih; Division 3 was led by Muqadam Mustafa; Division 4 was another commando division led by army officer Nassif. Each division was assigned to attack specific villages.

"They had a plan, if the Division1 was defeated, the commando's division should go to assist it in order to achieve the targeted plan. Amongst the villages attacked were Baza, Hassnpier, Dhie and a few more villages in the area.

"Later in the evening of 6th August 1988, an army division from the 72 Infantry Batallion headed towards a few villages in the area. Amongst them were a number of jash. The area was between Hassnpier and Dahie villages. The soldiers and their officers attacked all the civilians. They were hitting them with gun butts and sticks and kicking them as they tried to collect all the villagers in one place.

"A few soldiers did not like this. It was obvious from their facial expressions, but their senior officers ordered them. Amongst those distressed about the situation was Leith Muradi from the army security division, Shawqi, and another soldier from Fallujah who was crying. Umar was another soldier from Sammarra: he was very distressed and crying as though he'd had a fit. He could not stop crying, and tried to hide behind a tree, to not let anyone see him. They were crying for the villagers and their children as the soldiers were shooting them all.

"Most of the soldiers and army officers were savages who had no sympathy, and they were shooting all the innocent children and women, the old and the young. The villagers' men had their hands tied behind their backs. None of the villagers had any weapons and there was no way they could resist and defend themselves".

Kamal's friend, a Kurdish soldier, said: "I have seen with my own eyes: those innocent civilian villagers - old, young, children and women - were all being shot dead. All those defenceless civilians were being shot. I have seen so many being shot dead, their corpses scattered around. They shot everything, even animals, sheep, goats, cows and donkeys. There was no one or nothing spared, and the blood was streaming everywhere".

"As I was a Kurd myself", recounted another of Kamal's friends, "I could not say anything. I was very distressed but could not do anything to help anyone. I could not believe anything like that would ever happen. Sometimes, I was unsure about what I was seeing, was it a dream or reality? They attacked all those civilian villagers in the area between Dahouk, Sersang and as far as the Turkish border. The Iraqi army rounded up all the villagers. I saw so many villagers' children, men and women who had no way to escape. They were all shot dead".

"On 7th September 1988", explained Kamal, "the army brought many villagers to the army barracks from Dahie village. They brought many families; the men had their hands tied behind their backs. So many families with children, the scene was so distressful. I could not understand how those army officers could do that, to shoot so many and bring the rest. All those children and women were crying. The Iraqi army had no human feeling or sympathy. They were beating and kicking all those families with children and they killed so many of them. They were acting like savages. One of the Arab army sergeants turned to me and said, "Today, everything is in our hands, green and dry is burning together, nothing will be spared."

"The next days was one of looting and plunder, with no exceptions. It was like a feast for all the senior officers and the lower ranks down to the ordinary soldiers. They were so happy to collect all the 'booty'. They would take anything, even from the corpses. They checked for valuables such as watches, rings and anything of value. The Ba'athist party called this Anfal, 'the spoils of war'. What war? These were defenceless civilians who had no guns or weapons to fight back.

"The soldiers were searching all the men, women and children, asking them, 'Do you have any money? Give us what you have'. The whole army was busy, loading the booty into cars. They took the villagers' cars, tractors, and collected their herds and loaded them into lorries".

A few days later, Kamal explained, "I was on leave, going home from the area towards Mosul and, on the way, there were so many lorries full of booty, sheep herds and cattle. The army sold them cheap to the Arabs. Many Arabs came from Baghdad and the South of Iraq to buy cheap booty.

"One of those days, one of my colleagues from the town of Beiji, who was a mullah, a religious man, turned to me and asked, 'My friend you are a Kurd and I would like to ask you a question. I took a sheep from the village. I want to take it to my family and children: is that halal or haram?' He meant, was it legitimate by religious teaching, or not?"

Kamal replied to the mullah, "You are a religious man yourself, you know better than me. That is booty from other people's property - so how can it be halal?"

It was obvious: booty of the Anfal campaign reached all parts of South Iraq - Basra, Kut, Diwanyia, Nasriyia, Amara, Rumadi and every corner of the South. On another occasion, as Kamal said, "I saw a few soldiers who had a family album of one of the plundered villages, they were looking through it, mocking the family pictures, joking about it and laughing".

"On another occasion, before the army went to a village, they launched an intense bombardment with heavy weapons for about half an hour. When they were certain there was no danger, the soldiers were sent closer to the village, and suddenly a calor gas cannister exploded with a big bang. They all ran to shelter and lie low. They thought it was a bomb or a rocket-propelled grenade, but it was just calor gas exploding in the heat of the burning buildings.

"At the Dahie village, all the village men had their hands tied behind their backs. A woman came forward, and asked for the army leader. They found Kamal: he was the only one who could understand the woman. She told Kamal to ask the army leader, 'Why you have come to kill us and destroy our peace and our village? You are not brave, you tied our men's hands. They are only peasants, farmers and shepherds. If you are brave, untie their hands and give them weapons. Men should face men on the battlefield. If you are brave, untie their hands and fight them. This is not fair, why you are doing this to us?' Kamal interpreted what the woman said. The army leader had no reply".

Another day Kamal was with a group of soldiers in a village orchard with peaches, gauges, walnuts, figs and grapes. Amongst the soldiers, someone called Ali said, "Young men, eat whatever you like, but please do not take any trees. Today is ours, tomorrow will be theirs."

"It was so sad", recalled Kamal. "The assault was not only on humans, but also on all the animals, trees and orchards. Soldiers were using sharp knives to slice off walnut tree barks. They took the tree barks as souvenirs back to Baghdad and the South of Iraq. The tree barks were so beautiful, to use at home for a decor. It was so sad because, when the tree barks were sliced off, the tree would eventually die. They had no mercy for anything.

"Not even domestic animals spared. Many of them ran away and sheltered in the mountains. Whenever soldiers spotted any movement there, they shelled the area with artillery bombs and sent in army helicopters. Several times, they found horses, goats, donkeys and cows hiding in the caves. As soon as they saw anything, or suspected any movement in the mountains, they bombed the area. The army did not leave anything alone until they had killed it. A few villagers who escaped, came back and surrendered. I asked a man, 'Why did you come back?'

"'We could not go anywhere and couldn't go across the border to Turkey', the poor man replied. They surrendered to the army and, like the rest of the other villagers, they were murdered.

"I wonder if one day, we will have a truthful democracy and civil law and bring those criminals to face justice. Many of them are still at large. Those in charge of Federal Republic of Iraq, if they are true representatives of Iraqi people, they will find those who have taken part, and committed eight Anfal Campaigns from February to September 1988 and make them face the court of International Law.

"We will never have a true federal republic until those who committed crimes of Genocide and Race Killing face justice, so as to reinforce the true meaning of Mesopotamian civilisation and to give the people a restored faith in their Federal Republic".1

1.Hashtaw Hasht, number 5 & 6 2nd year 2006 page 224- 228

Genocide and the Banality of Evil

Peter Singer is one of the best living philosophers. He is known as a consequentialist philosopher, which means he believes that the best action is the one that produces the best results. And to work out the best result we need to take into account what is in the interests of all concerned, not only humans, but even also the interests of animals. What we can all see in the aftermath of this horror is that it was an Auschwitz-like campaign of genocide. We, all human beings and organisations of the international community, need to be alert and stick together for the sake of civilisation and to save the essence of humanity and prevent further crimes of genocide anywhere in the world.

The UN Declaration of 9th December 1948 was meant to prevent future race killings or genocide. However, the civilised world turned a blind eye to the Anfal Campaign and it was not interested in recognising campaigns of mass killings of civilian Kurds. It was also known that around 200 international companies provided Saddam's regime with funds and WMD technology. It was not only the superpowers that were silent and inept. The Muslim nations, especially the Arab League, were as well. In fact, many of them supported Saddam to his last breath, right up to his execution.

Many of those who committed crimes of mass murder and genocide are still at large. Few of these criminals have been prosecuted. Just like the German Nazi Adolf Eichmann, there must be a day when they will face justice.

Eichmann was a hardworking administrator. From 1942 he was in charge of transporting the Jews of Europe to concentration camps in Poland, including Auschwitz. This was part of Adolf Hitler's 'final solution'. Hitler's plan was to kill all the Jews living in the lands occupied by German forces. Eichmann was not directly responsible for the policy of systematic killing – it was not his idea. However, he was heavily involved in organising the railway system that made it possible.

This is similar to Saddam's Anfal campaign. Those who obeyed the orders for mass killings should face justice for crimes against humanity, for their role in the genocide campaign. Those in the Iraqi army, the security forces, and those whom the regime brought from other Arab countries to help execute about 200,000 Kurdish families and children – the people who committed these heinous crimes must, one day, face justice.

All the people who played vital roles in the massacres must be brought to trial, just like Eichmann, who initially escaped justice and fled to Buenos Aries, Argentina. Finally, Mossad, the Israeli secret police, tracked him down and arrested him. They brought him back to Israel, to stand trial and face justice.

The Ba'athists who took part in the mass killing of Kurds were like the German Nazis. They were like evil beasts and sadists who enjoyed other people's suffering.

The philosopher Hanna Arendt, (1905-1975), a German Jew who had immigrated to the United States, reported on Eichmann's trial for the New Yorker magazine. She was interested in coming face to face with a product of the Nazi totalitarian state, a society in which there was little room to think for individuals. She wanted to understand this man, get a sense of what he was like, and see how he could have done such terrible things.

Arendt had fled the Nazis herself, leaving Germany for France, but eventually becoming a US citizen. As a young woman at the University of Marburg, her teacher had been the philosopher Martin Heidegger. Eventually they became lovers and married, but later Heidegger turned out to be a Nazi himself, and so he left his wife.

Later in Jerusalem, Arendt was to meet a very different sort of Nazi.

Here was a rather ordinary man who chose not to think too much about what he was doing. His failure to think had disastrous consequences. He was something far more common but equally dangerous, an unthinking man. In a Germany where the worst forms of racism were written into the law, it was easy for him to persuade himself that what he was doing was right. Circumstances gave him opportunity for a successful career, and he took it.

 Hitler's Final Solution was an opportunity for Eichmann to do well, to show that he could do a good job. This is difficult to imagine, and many critics of Arendt would not think she was right, but she felt that he was sincere when he claimed to be doing his duty. He did not seem to have held any hatred towards Jews, unlike many other Nazis who were ready to beat a Jew to death.

During his trial he did not seem to show any remorse or sense of guilt. He simply thought he was an employee and had obeyed orders. When he was in charge of trains to send millions to the concentration camps, where Jews were systematically murdered in the gas chambers, he thought that there was nothing wrong with that, since he had not broken the law, and had never directly killed anyone, or asked for anyone to it for him. He had behaved reasonably.

There was no need for Eichmann to see people bundled into cattle trucks or to visit the death camps, so he did not commit any crime, he thought. There was a witness who told the court that Eichmann could not become a doctor because he was afraid of the sight of blood. Yet there was blood on his hands. He was the product of a system that had somehow prevented him from thinking critically about his own actions and the results they produced for real people. It was though he could not imagine other people's feelings at all. Arendt the philosopher used the term "banality of evil" to describe what she saw in Eichmann. Eichmann's ignorance of other people's suffering cost him his life

Arendt's philosophy was linked to recent history and lived experience. Her book, Eichmann in Jerusalem, was based on her observations of one man and the sort of language and justifications he gave in his trial. From what she saw in Eichmann's trial she developed a more general explanation of evil in a totalitarian state and its effects on those who did not resist its thought patterns. Eichmann failed to see how other people saw the situation and he failed to question the rules. He lacked imagination. Arendt described him as shallow and brainless.

Eichmann was obedient to immoral orders. In addition, obeying Nazi orders was, as far as Arendt was concerned, the same as supporting the Final Solution. 'That all Jews should be killed.' By failing to question what he told to do, and by carrying out those orders, he took part in mass murder, even though, from his point of view, he was just doing his train timetables. At one point of his trial, he even claimed to be acting according to Immanuel Kant's theory of moral duty – as if he had done the right thing by following orders. He completely failed to understand that Kant believed that treating human beings with respect and dignity was fundamental to morality.

For Peter Singer, the whole of question of morality is based on the idea of consistency: consistency in treating similar cases equivalently. Singer even defends the rights of animals against cruelty. However, we are still ignoring the treatment of human beings, including vulnerable children and elderly who are shot dead or buried alive in mass graves Many believe in the sanctity of human life - that is always wrong to kill another human being.

One can also never forget the destruction of the way of life, culture and environment of the Kurdish countryside and also the role of foreign companies and governments that supported and traded with

Saddam's regime and profited from his campaign of genocide. Their involvement in mass murder must not be hidden.

Providing information on the scale of the campaign of Genocide against the Kurds, we draw on material in 'Anfal Magazine' sponsored by the Kurdistan Regional Government's Ministry of Anfal.

Saddam's regime had a plan to either exterminate or relocate all Kurds from their own land that had been their home for at least the past 10,000 years. Saddam's regime saw this as its 'final solution' to the problem of Kurds demanding their basic human rights. The Ba'athist's answer was to slaughter, plunder and Arabise Kurds and Kurdish land, because they considered Kurdistan as the Eastern border of the Arab Nation.

On 4th June 2007 the mass murder of the Kurds was formally recognised as a crime of genocide by the new Federal Republic of Iraq. On 14th April 2008 the Iraqi parliament also specifically recognised Saddam's Anfal campaign and policy of ethnic cleansing as genocide.

Ever since, the Kurdistan Regional Government (KRG) has been trying to calculate the total number of Kurds murdered in Saddam's ethnic cleansing campaign. They have formed many teams of experts to research all the details. It has been estimated that more than 250,000 Kurds were killed and injured in Saddam's mass murder ethnic cleansing campaign. It is thought that millions have suffered from the long-term effects of physical and psychological injuries. The research is still underway because of the scale of this inhuman and murderous campaign, in which tens of thousands vanished without trace.

1.   The Man who didn't ask Questions by Hanna Arendt, p.208-214

And A Modern Gadfly by Peter Singer p.239

From Nigel Warburton, A Little History of Philosophy, published 2012

The Arabisation Campaigns

The decision to divide Kurdistan was made after the Ottoman Empire collapsed in 1918 and Iraq was founded by the British Empire as a state ruled by a Hashemite monarchy. The British gave a green light to the tribal Saudi nomads and subsequent Iraqi regimes to implement a policy of subjugation of the Kurds. The idea of Arabisation was integral to this.

It should have been inconceivable that an entire country, with its vast natural resources of water, petrol, gas and agricultural land would be left in the hands of uncultured tribal Arabs. Their patriarchal and despotic mentality soon came to the fore when Iraqi minister Yasin Hashemi brought the tribes of al Jibur and al Ubaid to the Kurdish Kirkuk area, settling them in the plain of Hawija. This development followed the discovery of oil in Kirkuk.

The Iraqi regime provided these nomadic tribes with agricultural education. Gradually Kurdish farmers were evicted, with little or no compensation, and forced to leave the area. The government created regulations to prevent them from returning to their ancestors' homeland.

In the following years of occupation, successive Iraqi regimes sought to minimise the Kurdish populations in the Kirkuk, Mosul, Sinjar, Jalawla, Baquba / Diala areas bordering the newly-established Arab areas of Iraq. These areas are known to this day as 'disputed territories'.

The policy of Arabisation in Kurdistan was applied in various ways. Kurdish education was initially restricted and eventually banned. All teaching was to be in Arabic. The government encouraged Kurdish children to study the Arabic language so as to undermine their own culture and language. They also designed policies to encourage Kurds to register as Arabs. The names of villages, towns and cultural institutions were gradually changed to Arabic: Kirkuk's name, for example, was changed to Tamim. They sought to glorify the Arab race, and created hatred between the two races.

The Ba'athists intensified the Arabisation campaign after they took power. In 1981, the regime gave 8000 stolen plots of Kirkuk land to newly-migrated Arab families whom the regime supported with jobs, grants to build houses and businesses grants.

On 6th September 2001 Saddam's revolutionary council proclaimed law number 199 stating that any Iraqi aged 18 or over was free to register as an Arab. This was an attempt to accelerate Arab domination of the disputed areas. Another Ba'athist policy was to encourage assimilation through intermarriage between Arabs and Kurds.

After the collapse of Saddam's regime, on 9th February, 2004 the head of the Patriotic Union of Kurdistan (PUK), Mam Jalal Talabani, produced a copy of an historical document at the Iraqi assembly. It had been approved by the League of Nations and said, "The border of Iraqi Arabs has never exceeded the 'Hamreen Mountain". This is a stretch of rocky mountains and hills near Tuz and south of Kirkuk. He produced another document recording a conversation between Winston Churchill, the United Kingdom prime minister during the Second World War, and Malik Faisal, king of Iraq, in which Churchill stated that the legitimate border between Arabs and Kurds was 'Jabal Hamreen.' Talabani called for the removal of the Arab tribes from the Arabised areas, including the plain of Hawija near Kirkuk.

Talabani also produced a historical document from the Dictionary of Information. This was the geography encyclopaedia of the Ottoman era. Printed and published in Istanbul in 1896, it said: "The city of Kirkuk is in the Mosul region, 160km South East of Mosul, situated in a hilly area in the Adham that includes Sharzour region. It has a population of 30,000, with a castle, 26 mosques, 15 schools of worship, 12 Khans / caravanserai, 1,282 shops, a hospital, a few handmade manufacturers and eight public baths". The report indicated that

75% of the city's population were Kurds and the rest consisted of Turkmens, Arabs, 760 Jews and 460 Childani Christians. This document was produced for a committee of Iraqi officials, headed by Dr Abdul Al Hamid and comprising Kurds, Arabs and Turcoman, set up to discuss the demography of Kirkuk. It confirmed that Kirkuk could not rightfully be separated from the Kurdistan Region.

It is clear that, even if the Kurds hadn't started an armed struggle and revolution, the policy of Arabisation, pursued over several decades, would still have happened.

The regime occupied the lands and houses of Kurdish villagers and city dwellers with threats of violence and murder by gangs of government criminals. These lands were occupied with little compensation, and properties were seized with no compensation. The government made local councils design roads that went through Kurdish properties. This kind of forced occupation was worse than what the Jews did to the Palestinians.

The regime brought in tribal Arabs to replace Kurds and provided them with employment and whatever resources they needed. The Arabs arrived with guns and they were also given employment in the security forces, with training designed to criminalise them and encourage more attacks on Kurds and their properties.

The regime started changing the borders of the Kurdish regions so as to shrink the overall size of the Kurdish areas. It also falsified the census reports in 1977, 1987 and 1997 so as to reduce the number of Kurds recorded as living in the disputed areas. 1

1.Hashtw Hasht, the seasonal Kurdish magazine, Slemani 2006 128 – 144

Genocide and Ethnocide

When a people is too numerous to be killed physically, the occupiers use cultural genocide and linguicide. What cannot be accomplished through physical genocide in one generation can be accomplished over several generations through cultural and linguistic genocide. This was seen in Kurdistan in the glorification of the occupiers' Arabic language by some religious, uneducated and gullible Kurds who often emphasise their views in everyday social discussions with heavily-accented formal Arabic expressions.

Cultural assimilation was the main objective of the occupying forces when they imposed their language in education and in work correspondence, and they banned Kurdish books, magazines and national ceremonies and celebrations. These draconian measures were aimed at killing off the cultural expression of the subjugated nation. The despotic regime of tribal Arabs in Iraq, whether Saudis or Iraqis, imposed their patriarchal culture with the aid of religion, used to fool people into accepting slavery and occupation, and with the assistance of their cronies from some religious and landowning families. 1

The regime pursued these policies across many area of life:

• In the public field: by destroying institutions of self-governance - for example, the removal of Slemani University.

• In the social field: by disrupting social cohesion, killing or removing important individuals such intellectuals and non-compliant religious leaders, and by stripping local elders who did not support the occupation of their roles in their communities. .

• In the cultural field: by prohibiting or destroying cultural institutions and activities, and by substituting vocational education for the liberal arts in order to prevent humanistic thinking which is dangerous because it promotes nationalistic ideals. Another method was to prevent Kurdish educational research and always put obstacles in the way of any arts, sports and educational initiatives.

• In the economic field: by shifting wealth to the occupying country and depriving people who did not accept the dominant Ideology of the Ba'athist regime of the right to work or trade. Between 1968 and 2003, only one of the 18 biggest private companies in Iraq was owned by a Kurd, and he was a regime crony.

• In the biological field: by a policy of depopulation, such as the deportation and relocation of thousands of villagers and destruction of their fields, orchards, cattle and all means of self-sufficiency. Nearly 5,000 villages were razed to the ground and the villagers were collected in round-the-clock guarded concentration camps.

• In the field of physical existence: by introducing a starvation rationing system and through the mass killings of the Barzani people, the chemical attack on Halabja and the eight stages of the Anfal genocide campaigns in which about 200,000 Kurds were massacred, with many buried alive.

• In the religious field: by interfering in the activities of the mosques, which provided religious and national leadership to Kurds.

• In the field of morality: by creating an atmosphere of moral debasement, through abuse, rape and providing venues for forced prostitution and immoral activities in detention centres and prisons - for example, in the Iraqi army, anyone who refused to implement orders was threatened with being raped while imprisoned.

According to Lemrik, the starvation caused by the destruction of economic life is not a consequence of revolution or war, but a conscious tactic of genocide. A daily struggle for bread may discourage thinking in both general and national terms. Saddam's regime did the same as the German Nazis who purposefully created conditions of malnutrition for the peoples of the occupied countries and especially those they were targeting, like the Jews, Poles and Slovenes. 2

Genocide has two aspects: the destruction of the national pattern of the target group and its replacement by the national pattern of the oppressing group. (Lemkin 1944, 79)

It is an extension of a long tradition of legal discrimination, and Hilberg summarises the phased deterioration of attitudes under the anti-Semitic administration of Nazi Germany: "You have no right to live among us as Jews. You have no right to live among us. You have no right to live." 3

.

The Iraqi regimes, and especially Saddam's regime, did the same, in so many shapes and forms, in their campaigns of genocide against Kurds.

Genocide is an advanced form of state terrorism, a coordinated use of force by the elite within a society to maintain or extend its power over the targeted group, which is perceived as a threat, within the same state. Examples of states that have followed the same pattern of committing the crime of genocide include the Soviet Union and former Czarist Russia, and the Turkish Republic and former the Ottoman Empire. Bauman sees the absence of democracy as the most important factor enabling genocide to occur. 4

Massacres do not happen by coincidence. They are usually the last step in a long process of oppression and take place when the oppressor has suffered important military defeats. For example, the Armenian genocide started after the Turkish defeat in Bulgaria in 1912, and the killing of Jews intensified after the Nazi defeat at Stalingrad in 1943; most of the Jews were killed after Germany had actually lost the war. 5

Genocide has two important structural dimensions: It represents a systematic effort over time to liquidate a national population, usually a minority, and it functions as a fundamental political policy to ensure conformity and participation by the citizenry. Like Lemkin, Bauman also says that genocide is rarely aimed at the total annihilation of a group; rather, the purpose of the violence is to destroy the targeted group as a viable community capable of self-perpetuation and defence of its self-identity.

The objective of violence is usually reached when the level of violence has been great enough to undermine the will of the sufferers, and make them accept the given orders, and when the targeted group has been deprived of the resources necessary to continue the struggle - as happened in Kurdistan in 1975 with the Algiers pact.

The objective of genocide is that the marked group, once deprived of its leadership and centres of authority, will lose its cohesiveness and the ability to sustain its identity. The inner structure of the group will collapse, and its members may have no option but to assimilate, one by one, into the new structure, or be forcibly reassembled into a new category. 6

Lemkin did not use the term cultural genocide, but he recognised that Hitler had different population policies and aims in the occupied areas, some of which were to be 'Germanised' and assimilated with cultural discrimination being one method to achieve this. Lemkin did not call this process genocide, but a policy of forced assimilation that he termed cultural genocide. (Fein 1993, 8-11)

Vakakn Dadrian distinguishes between five types of genocide:

- Cultural genocide, in which the aim is assimilation.

- Latent genocide, the result of unintended consequences such as civilian deaths during bombing raids, or the accidental spread of disease during an invasion.

• Retributive genocide, designed to punish a segment of a minority - as was the case with the Barzani civilians, more than 8000 of whom were shot dead or buried alive in South Iraq.

• Utilitarian genocide, using mass killing to obtain economic resources - that was the case with the Garmyian Anfal campaign, aimed at clearing the area for Arab tribes to settle there, and in the Kirkuk area, where the objective was to gain oil resources.

• Optimal genocide, the mass killing of members of a group to achieve its total obliteration, as in the Armenian and Jewish holocausts. The chemical attack on Balisan valley and Halabja in March 1988 and the eight stages of Anfal campaign also took this shape. 7

.

Cultural genocide is also called ethnocide. It is the deliberate elimination of a group's collective memory, identity, or culture without its physical elimination. It includes attacks on political and social institutions, culture, language, national feelings, religion, and on the economic existence of the group. 8

Social science is one way of understanding the change from traditional to modern, where, for example 'tribalism' has been replaced by nationalist ideas. Preventing research about the minority group can be one method used by the majority to prevent the minority from developing a 'modern' way of thinking, because it is not possible to understand properly the present situation without knowing its background. By preventing research about a minority, the majority can keep it traditional while it develops its own society in a modern way. In the Kurdish context, this means that, if there had been a proper understanding among the Kurds about their tribal system, it might have been easier for them to overcome the lack of unity that the system had caused. 9

1.(Skutnabb-Kangas and Bucak 1994, 366, 367, Skutnabb-Kangas and Philipson 1991)

.Kristina Koivunem, The invisible War in South Kurdistan, KRG publication 2005 140, 141

2. (Hilberg 1961, 101-105, Lemkin 1944, 85) Kristiina Koivunen, the Invisible War in North Kurdistan 2005, 29

3. (Bauman 1989, 1-2; Hilberg 1961, 3-4) Kristiina Koivunen, the Invisible War in North Kurdistan 2005, 30.

4.(Horowitz 1997, 35-36)

5. (Hilberg 1961, 4; Horowitz 1987, 65) Kristiina Koivunen, The Invisible War in North Kurdistan 2005, 30.

6. (Bauman 1989, 119; Hitchcock and Twedt 1995, 49-492; Horowitz 1997, 20-21) Kristiina Koivunen, the Invisible War in North Kurdistan 2005, 31

7. (Dadrian1975, ref Johonson and Chalk 1987, 9) Kristiina Koivunen, the Invisible War in North Kurdistan 2005, 32.

8. (Van Bruinessen 1994a, 166-167, Fein 1992, 2-4; Jonassohn 1992, 21; Jonassohn and Chalk 1987, 8)

9.Kristiina Koivunen, The Invisible War in North Kurdistan 2005, page 35, 36

Philosophy and the Way of Life in the Revolution

To help understand how 30 million Kurds have been unfairly treated by the international community, we may consider the great works of famous philosophers and see how the viewpoint of these humanist thinkers might apply to the situation.

Plato believed that only philosophers understand what the world is truly like. They discover the nature of reality by thinking rather than relying on their senses. He also thought that all is not as it seems. There is a significant difference between appearance and reality. Most of us mistake appearance for reality. We think we understand, but we do not. However, Kurds would not be able to believe and see as Plato did, because the denial of their basic human rights by the colonial policy of ethnocide meant they were not allowed to properly educate themselves and develop their own culture and history.

Philosophy shows the value of learning, understanding and seeing the reality of what is really going on around us and how our life, culture, economy are affected. This prompts us to stand up for our rights and fight to the death to preserve our existence. Despite all the prohibition and enslavement, Kurds did rise up on many occasions to seek their human rights, just as modern and ancient philosophies have urged us to do.

*A Little History of Philosophy by Nigel Warburton 2011 (library Code 190)

Wisdom for Socrates was not in knowing many facts, or knowing how to do things. It meant understanding the true nature of our existence, including the limits of what we can know. Despite being barred from learning many facts and the essence of being subjugated, Kurds did not lack an understanding of their situation, which was why they never gave up, as often they preferred death to enslavement.

IBID P.3

For Aristotle, "true happiness is in success, not in temporary worldly pleasure". If people think children are happy, they are not, as they have not lived long enough yet. A true success lies in finding out and knowing, to serve humanity, and to expose the savagery of regimes like Saddam's and those who created them. Success lies in serving humanity. Life is nothing without success; that was how the peshmargas lived, standing up for their rights, and the rights of their fellow compatriots. One could see whether they were truly happy or not, as they defiantly and triumphantly walked to the hanging loop of execution.

The point of moderate philosophical scepticism is to get closer to the truth, or at least to reveal how little we know or can know. This might be true for a while, but when we ignore the reality of what is going on, we are bound to accept subjugation, and eventually lose our freedom and our awareness of the need to defend our existence. We should bear unhappiness and suffer for the sake of final freedom. Suffering is a part of life, and we can get used to suffering, as many peshmagas did when they endured freezing cold seasons, lack of sleep, hunger and torture, and they fought and died for the sake of freedom.

Although not all peshmargas were well-educated, through observing everyday events, they felt the suffering of ordinary people, many of whom were in no position to fight back. Therefore, they volunteered to put their lives at stake for the sake of others' happiness: that was the true meaning of being a peshmarga.

Physical pain can be made bearable by remembering past pleasures of fighting back. This often applied when peshmargas were caught wounded and then subjected to continuous torture in prison, but they did not give in, refused to reveal any information and died at the hands of their torturers. (Remember Wasta Anwar, the master builder from Halabja).

Emotions influence reasoning and damage our judgement; we should not just control them, but remove them whenever possible. The mind can remain free even when the body is enslaved. This was the situation of our political prisoners, who were ready to die and not surrender to oppression. It was emotionally difficult to know what was happening, but emotional reactions would lead to disaster, while reason would reveal that the occupiers were the enemies of humanity. Therefore one had to control one's own emotions and not to give in to spontaneity. That was how Zoran controlled his emotions when seeing so much unfairness before he went to the mountains. Pitying oneself is a road to disaster.

• Boethius, 476-525, Rome, on the consolation of philosophy:

Happiness can only come from the inside, from things that human beings can control, not from anything that bad luck can destroy. The message is that riches, power, and honour are worthless since they can come and go. No one should base their hopes on such a fragile foundation. Happiness should come from something that is more solid, something that cannot be taken away. Some

Kurdish mercenaries gave in to the lure of money, good jobs, positions and other temporary material interests. These were trivial possessions, and the nation's dignity and integrity was undermined because of their greed. True happiness is much bigger and much more valuable: it is to own your home, your country and to be the master of your own destiny.

- Niccolo Machiavelli 1469-1527 Florence, Italy:

An effective leader must act like a beast to learn where the foxes and lions are. Human beings are greedy, dishonest and unreliable. It is dangerous to trust anyone to keep their promises unless they are terrified of the consequences of not keeping them.

This kind of leadership was needed in Kurdistan, because the revolution required a system of discipline and agreed responsibilities in which everyone gave priority to the main purpose of the struggle. Enemies were trying to penetrate the revolution by any means so as to create doubt, suspicion and distrust amongst the revolutionaries. Therefore, a strong leader was needed to stand up and fight back by leading the revolution with the true peshmarga spirit.

- Thomas Hobbes, 1588–1679, England's greatest political thinker (and a fitness fanatic):

Life outside society would be "solitary, poor, nasty, brutish, and short". Individuals in the state of nature, then, had very good reasons for wanting to work together and seek peace; it was the only way they could be protected. Without that, their lives would be terrible; safety was far more important than freedom. Fear of death would drive people towards forming a society. People would agree to give up quite a lot of freedom in order to make a social contract with each other.

In Kurdistan the revolution created a tendency for the majority of people to become revolutionaries in one way or another, whether or not they belonged to a political party, because the insecurities of life required social and political togetherness. The community shared many things for the sake of security. This created cohesion for the sake of protecting freedom, and so everyone would be ready to bow to the community's rules. That was how a society with a spirit of fighting back was forged.

- Baruch Spionza, 1632-1677, the Netherlands:

Free will is an illusion. There is no spontaneous free action at all. A stone thrown in the air, if it could become conscious might imagine it is moving through its own will power, but it isn't.

There wasn't simply a free will to form a Kurdish political party or for a tribal group to stand up for their rights. Instead there was a necessity, arising from the terrible experiences of being enslaved and bartered with by the occupiers. That was why unity and togetherness was important. The revolution was not a natural phenomenon, like a natural disaster: it came from oppression. There was no escape: people had to stand up in order to protect themselves, their families, their relatives, neighbours and eventually their nation. That was how common fears, insecurities and the quest for survival created a nation and an urge among the Kurds to fight to the death to protect their land and way of life.

• John Locke, 1632-1704, England, champion of religious tolerance:

It is absurd to try to force people to change their religious beliefs through torture. We have a God-given right to life, freedom, happiness and property. This thinking influenced the Founding Fathers who wrote the Constitution of the United States of America.

This thinking could be applied when the Ba'athist regime started its campaign of Ba'athification. This political belief system was like a religion, and force was applied to try and change peoples' allegiances. Kurds were pressured to join a chauvinist, pan-Arab nationalist party, and to become Arabs or mercenaries of the tribal Arab occupiers. This led many young people to fight back, to take up arms and go to the mountains.

• Voltaire, 1694-1778, France, a witty, brave man, champion of free speech and religious tolerance:

"I hate what you say but defend to the death your right to say it".

Voltaire's stance on democracy was that people should be open-minded and allow different views, political doctrines, religions and social conduct – even those they might not feel comfortable with – to be expressed. Individual freedom is the root of a true democratic system.

• Jean-Jacques Rouseau, 1712-1778:

An individual living within a state can be both free and obey the laws of the state. Free Will and General Will can dialectically combine. General Will represents the will of the people, which should be sovereign for the good of all.

This applies to the true principles of democracy. One's free will should be within the democratic framework of the whole system and therefore one has to obey the rules, and may have to give away some rights, for the sake of keeping together the whole.

During the revolution, nationalist feeling became so powerful that it was almost like a religion which no one would dare to defy. Such strong feelings led to many mistakes being made, because no one could criticize the revolution. This was exploited by the occupiers and led to internal conflict on many occasions.

Sajid and Rauf read many books and they were saddened by studying history because the world seemed so wicked and miserable. As Voltaire says, "After all history is but a chronicle of crime and misery. The host of innocent and peace loving people always disappears from view in this vast theatre, while the chief actors are nothing but evil and ambitious men".

From, A Little History of Philosophy by Nigel Warburton 2012

Pages: Aristotle, 1 - 9 Boethius, 40 – 46 Nicolo Machiavelli 51 – 57 Thomas Hobbs, 57 – 62 Baruch Spionza, 76 – 81 John Lock, 81 - 87 Voltaire 93 – 99 Jean Jacques Rousseau105 - 110

Some Conclusions

It is clear from looking back at the history of the Middle East that Kurdistan has been divided for the strategic reasons of various 'superpowers'. When new authoritarian regimes were founded by Britain and France after the First World War, territories were left in the hands of minority ethnic groups: in Iraq the Sunni minority held sway, while in Syria the Shia minority dominated. The political structure of the Middle East was based on racial, ethnic, cultural and religious divisions, and these differences have caused a permanent volatility, making peace and stability almost impossible.

The occupiers used many tools of domination including religion, ideology (communism, socialism), class (tribal feudalism), and even the façade of democracy. The despotic regimes used religious families and landowners to help them deprive the Kurds, Armenians, Shias, Christians and other religious sects and national minorities of their cultural, linguistic and basic human rights.

A policy of low-intensity warfare was imposed on all the subject minorities, especially the Kurds, leading to occasional uprisings and revolutions since 1921. The destruction of villages and the Kurds' traditional way of life amounted to ethnocide or the destruction of their culture and environment.

Another method of low-intensity warfare was censorship imposed to minimise international attention and suppress news of repression and mass murder.

One of the policies of the dictators was to prevent people from using their own language. Poor education provision and low literacy levels made a majority of the subject populations less aware of the reality of their situation. That meant many would stay reactionary and tribal in their outlook. As Plato says, "Ordinary people have little idea about reality because they are content with looking at what is in front of them rather than thinking deeply about it, but the appearances are deceptive. What they see are shadows, not reality".

After the First World War, the allied forces used religion when they put members of the Sunni Hashemite family in power in many parts of the Middle East for their own political and strategic purposes. The superpowers' own interests often influenced the actions of the League of Nations and subsequently of the United Nations. In January 1926, the League demanded that the civil rights of Kurds be observed, but this was never followed up or monitored.

After the downfall of the Iraqi monarchy, both the West and the Soviet Union interfered in Iraqi affairs.

The Soviet Union used the Iraqi Communist Party to support the new Iraqi Republic, and then it encouraged the Ba'athist regime to militarise Iraq by spending billions of dollars of Iraqi oil money on its weapons.

The arms trade fuelled corruption while, through sanctions, the Iraqi regime decreased the level of staple foods available to the Kurdish population. Governments, international companies and traders all benefited from the wars: peace meant the end of a profitable business.

Kurds tried to exploit political and historical conflicts between the different regimes – notably between Iraq and Iran and Syria and Iraq – to their advantage. However, none of these regimes wanted a just solution for the Kurds anywhere. Even if any Iraqi regime had ever intended to find a settlement to the Kurdish problem, other neighbouring countries would have created obstacles, because any solution would have encouraged Kurds to demand their rights in Turkey, Syria and Iran. Solving the Kurdish problem would have also had an adverse effect on the superpowers' strategic interests in the area.

Kurds in Iraq often blamed themselves and their leaders for their sorry situation. Indeed it is true that, prior to the Aylul revolution, uprisings and revolutions were dominated by religious leaders and landowners who were more pious than nationalist, easily manipulated by the Arabs and Turks and had vested interests in keeping the majority of Kurds in a state of illiterate ignorance.

Another mistake was that we Kurds always fought on our own doorstep and this contributed to the destruction of the Kurdish economy and traditional culture and way of life. We did not sufficiently take the fight to our enemy's land, as Zoran did. Our political leaders also lacked the vision required to unify the people and overcome, rather than foster, internal differences.

Our parties ignored other ways of fighting their enemies, including in the areas of education, learning, business, politics and technology. Even when despotic regimes supressed the revolution in Kurdistan, It was possible for Kurds to promote their cause abroad, where many lived in exile, especially in Europe and the United States. Our political parties failed to cooperate effectively abroad and develop an international profile for Kurds like that attained by the Palestinians and black South Africans.

 After the 1991 uprising, Kurds managed, with Western backing, to exclude Saddam's authority from the region. There was a double-burden of sanctions, Kurdistan's infrastructure was destroyed by the years of conflict and many people were left

without electricity or water. Despite these problems
- and the terrible misfortune of an internal civil war
in the 1990s - Kurds managed to establish order and
then enjoy oil-based economic expansion. Regular
parliamentary elections, although not always
perfect, were held. The region has until recently
enjoyed relative calm compared to the rest of Iraq
and the Middle East.

Today Kurds face a new existential challenge from
ISIS, the genocidal jihadist movement which includes
in its ranks former senior Ba'athist army officers.
Our political leaders must show heightened
statesmanship and always put the peoples' interests
before their own and their political parties'. This is a
dangerous time when Turks, Arabs and Iranians will
want us to fight each other, to create internal
conflict and destroy our KRG. It is a testing time,
demanding vigilance and unity.

There are many positive features of Kurdish culture,
mirroring the southern African concept of 'ubuntu'
or human kindness. There is the spirit of
cooperation, sharing anxieties and standing together
in facing enemies. There is also the enduring spirit of
hospitality: despite the still-fresh memories of Anfal,
we are today sheltering hundreds of thousands of
Arab refugees. Our society must always embody
these ancient values and emulate the best aspects

of our traditional, self-sufficient way of life in the mountains.

The KRG should concentrate on reviving agricultural production, so we can once again feed ourselves and not be dependent on Baghdad's petrol money. Our autonomy is useless without economic autonomy.

Over the past quarter-century, we have proven to the world we can govern ourselves, defend our land and withstand terrorism. It is vital that the international community back Kurdistan - a true example of Mesopotamian civilization in the Middle East - by all means. It is essential to do politics with our neighbours but, based on historical experience, we can never trust them. While full Independence remains our goal, it would be suicidal in current circumstances to declare it unilaterally, without the backing of the EU, USA and UN.

www.ingramcontent.com/pod-product-compliance
Lightning Source LLC
Chambersburg PA
CBHW061754250726

48657CB00001B/124